D1171877

FRIEDA LAWRENCE AND HER CIRCLE

Also by Harry T. Moore

THE PRIEST OF LOVE: A LIFE OF D. H. LAWRENCE
THE COLLECTED LETTERS OF D. H. LAWRENCE
  (*editor*)
HENRY JAMES AND HIS WORLD (*with F. W. Roberts*)
E. M. FORSTER
THE WORLD OF LAWRENCE DURRELL (*editor*)
SELECTED LETTERS OF RAINER MARIA RILKE (*editor*)

Frieda Lawrence, by the late Charles McKinley

FRIEDA LAWRENCE AND HER CIRCLE

Letters from, to and about
Frieda Lawrence

edited by
Harry T. Moore
and
Dale B. Montague

ARCHON BOOKS
Hamden, Connecticut

First published 1981 by
THE MACMILLAN PRESS LTD
London and Basingstoke
and in the U.S.A. as an Archon Book
an imprint of
THE SHOE STRING PRESS INC.
995 Sherman Avenue
Hamden, Connecticut 06514

Printed in Hong Kong

Library of Congress Cataloging in Publication Data

Lawrence, Frieda von Richthofen, 1879–1956.
Frieda Lawrence and her circle.

Includes index.
1. Lawrence, Frieda von Richthofen,
1879–1956. 2. Lawrence, David Herbert,
1885–1930—Biography—Marriage.
3. Authors, English—20th century—Biography.
4. Wives—England—Correspondence. I. Moore,
Harry Thornton. II. Montague, Dale B.
III. Title.
PR6023.A93Z5332 1981 823′.912 [B] 80–36766
ISBN 0–208–01886–7

Contents

Frieda Lawrence   *frontispiece*
Acknowledgements   vi
Introduction   vii

1. Letters between Frieda Lawrence and
   Edward W. Titus   1
2. Letters between Frieda Lawrence and Caresse
   Crosby   38
3. Letters from Frieda Lawrence and Ada Lawrence
   Clarke to Martha Gordon Crotch   42
4. Letters from Angelo Ravagli to Martha Gordon
   Crotch   71
5. Letters between Frieda Lawrence and Richard
   Aldington   73

Epilogue   138
Index   140

Acknowledgements

Our first acknowledgement must go to Mr Gerald Pollinger, Director of Laurence Pollinger Ltd, which deals with matters concerned with the Lawrence Estate. When Mr Pollinger learned of the existence of the letters included in this volume, he suggested that they be prepared for publication. We are also extremely indebted to Dr Warren Roberts, former Director of the Humanities Research Center at the University of Texas, who has permitted us to use the letters of Richard Aldington to Frieda Lawrence. To Dr Kenneth Peterson, Dean of Libraries at Southern Illinois University, we owe great thanks for his permission to use the Frieda Lawrence–Edward Titus correspondence from the Southern Illinois Library Archives, as well as the Caresse Crosby correspondence, with further thanks to Mr David Koch, Rare Books Librarian at that institution. The Titus letters are published by permission of his family, obtained by the Massachusetts rare-books dealer, Mr George Robert Minkoff. The Frieda Lawrence–Ada Lawrence Clarke letters belong to Harry T. Moore, and the Ada Clarke letters are printed here with the permission of Ada Clarke's son, Mr Herbert Clarke. We are also grateful to Mrs Hazel Guggenheim McKinley for permitting us to use a letter from Frieda to her, as well as a reproduction of the painting by her husband, the late Charles McKinley.

HARRY T. MOORE
DALE B. MONTAGUE

Introduction

She is ripping—she's the finest woman I've ever met—you
must above all things meet her. . . . She's the daughter of
Baron von Richthofen, of the ancient and famous house of
Richthofen—but she's splendid, she is really.

> D. H. Lawrence to Edward Garnett,
> 17 April 1912

In 1914, Lawrence married her, and she remained his wife
until his untimely death from tuberculosis at the age of
forty-four. They had their quarrels, mostly on the surface, but
Frieda's vitality contributed greatly to the vividness of all his
writing.

The coalminer's son, who had given up teaching in a
London suburb in 1912 because of his poor health, fell in love
with Frieda Weekley-Richthofen, wife of one of Lawrence's
former teachers at Nottingham University, where he had
been a scholarship student. He did not meet Frieda until after
he had left the university, and in 1912 accompanied her to
Germany; she stayed with him despite the fact that she had
three small children, and she and Lawrence journeyed across
the world as he wrote his many novels, stories, essays and travel
books. Lawrence died at Vence, in southern France, in 1930;
the letters in this volume depict her subsequent life.

This is perhaps sufficient background for the present
volume; for those unacquainted with the Lawrence–Frieda
story, it is told elsewhere in Harry T. Moore's *The Priest of
Love: A Life of D. H. Lawrence* (1974, 1977) and in the brilliantly
edited compilation of memoirs by those who knew Lawrence,
Edward Nehls's three-volume *Composite Biography* (1957–9).
Frieda's own lively account of the adventure of her life with

Lawrence is given in her *Not I, But the Wind* . . . (1954, 1976). We also have E. W. Tedlock's superbly edited volume of Frieda's *Memoirs and Correspondence* (1961, 1964). There are numerous books on the subject, including the first full biography of Frieda by Robert Lucas (1972). Aldous Huxley's early one-volume edition of *The Letters of D. H. Lawrence* (1932) and Harry T. Moore's two-volume set of *The Collected Letters of D. H. Lawrence* (1962) will be supplanted by the eight-volume edition now in preparation at the Cambridge University Press. It is amazing that a man who lived to be only forty-four years old, who was always frail, who suffered from tuberculosis, could write so many letters, most of which stand beside those of Keats as the finest in English. It is all the more amazing in that Lawrence also wrote some of the greatest novels of the modern world (including *Sons and Lovers, The Rainbow and Women in Love*), many first-rate short stories, and some of its finest poems (including 'Snake', 'The Ship of Death' and 'Bavarian Gentians'), as well as many brilliant essays and several superb travel books. But his income was meagre; it improved in the last two years of his life, after the underground success of his privately printed novel, *Lady Chatterley's Lover*, about which the present volume tells a great deal in its opening section.

II

This book is divided into five sections, the first of them comprising the exchange of letters between Frieda and the American Edward W. Titus (husband of the cosmetician Helena Rubinstein), who brought out a special edition of *Lady Chatterley* in Paris in 1929; the book had first appeared in Florence the year before, under the auspices of G. A. Orioli who, like Titus, plays an important part in the letters printed in this volume.

At least one letter from Lawrence to Titus remains, from 16 August 1929, two months after Titus had issued *Lady Chatterley*; this letter is already in print in Gerald Lacy's recent important edition of Lawrence's novella *The Escaped Cock*, which was first published by the Black Sun Press in Paris in 1928, and countless times since, under the bowdlerised name of *The Man who Died*; the Lacy edition was brought out by the

Black Sparrow Press of Santa Barbara, California, in 1973. The Lawrence letter to Titus is not repeated here because it is full of sales talk and statistics, an unusually dead letter for Lawrence to have written. Our first letter to Titus here, then, is one from Frieda written on 5 February 1930, the day before she took Lawrence from their house at Bandol in the South of France to the sanatorium at Vence, Alpes Maritimes; even in his most desperate illnesses, Lawrence had avoided sanatoria, and he left the one at Vence on 1 March, the day before he died. Titus was one of the few who attended the funeral at the cemetery at Vence, where Lawrence lay buried for five years under a gravestone with his principal symbol, the phoenix, patterned upon it with coloured stones. The removal of his body to America is discussed in later sections of this volume.

The first chapter of the book fortunately has the letters of both correspondents, always a great advantage in a volume of this kind. Titus not only conducted the Minikin Bookshop in Paris, but was also an *avant-garde* publisher both of books and of the magazine, *This Quarter*. His exchange of letters with Frieda contains little about Lawrence himself, but it is both dramatic and amusing as Frieda plays a cat-and-mouse game with Lawrence's surviving manuscripts.

These Frieda–Titus letters would make a book in themselves, but fortunately we have several other sets of correspondence which are perhaps even more interesting.

The second section of this collection represents letters between Frieda and Caresse Crosby, whose husband killed himself in New York in 1929. Their Black Sun Press in Paris had published Lawrence's *The Escaped Cock*, and eventually the two women quarrelled over ownership of the original manuscript.

The third set of letters in this book represents two women writing to a third. Frieda is, of course, one of the women and Lawrence's younger sister, Ada Lawrence Clarke, is the other. The third, whose letters are not available, is Martha Gordon Crotch, who for many years operated the Peasant Pottery Shop at Vence, where Lawrence died. She did not meet Frieda until after that event.

In the preceding year, 1929, twelve uniformed art critics from Scotland Yard invaded the Warren Gallery in London, during an exhibition of Lawrence's pictures there, and marched off with thirteen of them under the charge of obscenity. The paintings were neatly defended in court, and in Parliament questions were raised as to the propriety of the seizure; the prosecution even wanted to have the paintings burned. But they were released under an agreement that they be shipped to Lawrence, now so ill in southern Europe. After Martha Gordon Crotch became a friend of Frieda's she agreed to display them in her shop, where many of us first saw them.

'Auntie' Crotch was a fascinating character whom Norman Douglas used to call Martha of Hartlepool. She had come to southern France to die, after an operation in England which did her no good. During a later operation in France, a doctor discovered that the British surgeon, before sewing her up, had left his forceps inside her; these were removed, and she lived on to be eighty-nine. At her shop in Vence, she would proudly display the rust-furred forceps.

'Auntie' became the friend not only of Frieda, but also of Ada Lawrence Clarke, who lived with her husband and two sons in Ripley, Derbyshire. In her letters to 'Auntie', the reader can soon see Ada's affection for Frieda turning into hostility. Ada apparently tried to make no claim on the Lawrence Estate, but her older brother and sister, George and Emily (Mrs Needham) did so, and in 1932 the matter went to court in London. *Lady Chatterley* had brought in a good deal of money, despite the cheats who printed what are called pirated editions; but in 1932 no one could foresee that, after Lawrence's fame began to swell following the Second World War, the royalties would become enormous.

In any event, the letters both Frieda and Ada wrote to 'Auntie' Crotch provide a highly interesting footnote to modern literary history.

The fourth part of this volume consists of two letters from Angelo Ravagli who was in 1935 living with Frieda at the Lawrences' ranch at Taos, New Mexico. Frieda sent Ravagli to Vence to exhume and cremate Lawrence: Ravagli's experiences in carrying out this project tell of only a few of the difficulties he encountered.

III

The fifth section of this book is the longest and, in many ways, the most absorbing. Again we are fortunate in having both sides of a correspondence, this one covering more years than the earlier ones in this book. Here Frieda exchanges letters with one of Lawrence's oldest friends and, in the times when Lawrence's reputation was low, one of his sturdy defenders: Richard Aldington.

He had first met the Lawrences at a reception for the imagist poets in Amy Lowell's suite in the Berkeley Hotel in Piccadilly on the eve of the First World War. Aldington was then married to the American poet, Hilda Doolittle (who wrote as H. D.); he served in the war as an officer, was severely 'shell-shocked' as the phrase used to go, and in 1929 he brought out one of the significant novels of that conflict, particularly notable for its satiric element: *Death of a Hero*. As the letters to Frieda show, Aldington went to the United States during the Second World War, with his second wife Netta and their small daughter Catherine; they lived principally in Washington, D. C., and Florida, and drove west to the Lawrence ranch at Taos, New Mexico, moving on then to Los Angeles. After the war they lived in southern France. Aldington continued to write poetry and novels, with little financial success, and made some important translations. He aroused the ire of Norman Douglas's admirers (not too many of them to begin with) with his combined biography of Douglas and G. A. ('Pino') Orioli, *Pinorman* (1954); the following year he attracted widespread hatred—and extreme venom—with his *Lawrence of Arabia: A Biographical Inquiry*. All of this is discussed in the correspondence in the present volume.

(The foregoing suggests several comments. First of all, in 1977, one of the most notable British historians, Professor Hugh Trevor-Roper, then of Oxford, said in the *New York Times* that Lawrence of Arabia was a fake and that he was surprised that people had not noted this when Aldington's exposé came out in 1955. Another comment: Miriam J. Benkovitz in 1975 brought out a large volume of Aldington letters and is now collaborating with Norman T. Gates on a collected edition; Harry T. Moore and Ian S. MacNiven are bringing out two other books of Aldington letters, one of them his exchange of letters with Lawrence Durrell, the other continuing the letters between Aldington and Ezra Pound. Also, a Canadian professor, Charles Doyle, is writing the authorised biography of Aldington.)

IV

The editors of this book have tried to make reading it as easy as possible by generally avoiding those bottom-of-the-page footnotes, which so often bring the eyes rushing downstairs to find no one at the door. Sometimes when only part of a name is mentioned, we have made it clear in brackets (not too distracting, we hope), giving the rest of the name; occasionally books referred to without being named are treated in the same way, if we definitely know what book is in the writer's mind. And we have occasionally added a footnote for a quick reference to someone or something that needs a brief identification.

All the letters in this collection are reproduced here with minimal alteration. The original spelling and punctuation has been retained as far as possible, though for the sake of clarity the layout of the letters has been standardised. Single quotation marks have been used throughout, and a few misspelled proper names have been silently corrected.

We have also felt that people well known in the literary world need no special identification—John Middleton Murry, Katherine Mansfield, Norman Douglas, Michael Arlen, Sir Compton Mackenzie, Witter Bynner, and various others. But we will here provide some data about various figures less familiar. Of course everyone who knows the Lawrence area will know who the man is whom the various correspondents refer to as Angelo, Angelino or Angie: this is the previously mentioned Angelo Ravagli, an Italian army officer who, not long after Lawrence's death, accompanied Frieda on her first return to the Lawrence ranch above Taos; some years later, Angelo Ravagli married Frieda and, after her death in 1956, returned to his family in Italy. He died there in 1975.

The name Frere or Frere Reeves keeps recurring; this was A. S. Frere Reeves (later A. S. Frere, for many years the principal director of the London publishing house of William Heinemann Ltd, who, after Lawrence's death, helped Frieda greatly, as he also helped Aldington). Frere's wife, Pat, is mentioned at least once; she was a London journalist, daughter of the writer of mysteries, Edgar Wallace.

'Kot' is the Russian-born translator, S. S. Koteliansky, a good friend of Lawrence's though hardly of Frieda's. Mabel is Mabel Dodge Luhan, 'Empress of Taos', who first invited the Lawrences there; 'Brett' is the Hon. Dorothy Brett, who in 1924 went with the Lawrences on one of their return journeys to New Mexico and remained there, becoming renowned as a painter of the local Indians and their ceremonies. She died in New Mexico in 1978 at ninety-three. The Miriam whom Frieda occasionally refers to is the origin of the character so named in Lawrence's *Sons and Lovers*; her actual name was Jessie Chambers. Aldington now and then mentions F.-J. Temple, a writer and radio executive in southern France. Jacob Zeitlin is a Los Angeles bookseller. Alister Kershaw is perhaps the best friend Aldington ever had; as Aldington's literary executor he has done much to help along the reawakening interest in that author. 'Nusch' is the nickname of Frieda's sister Joanna. Ottoline is Lady Ottoline Morrell, owner of Garsington, a vast estate in Oxfordshire and the original of the rather fantastic character Hermione in Lawrence's *Women in Love*. The Arabella whom Frieda occasionally mentions to Edward Titus is undoubtedly the American Dorothy Yorke, one-time companion of Aldington and known in the Lawrence circle as Arabella.

Some of these letters contain attacks on various people. The harsh words Frieda early uses about Laurence Pollinger were made when he was with the firm of literary agents, Curtis Brown Ltd, which handled Lawrence's writings in the later years of his life and for a time afterwards; later, when Pollinger set up his own agency, he and Frieda were devoted friends; she trusted him completely and spoke well of him—and indeed, in the Lawrence revival he handled Lawrence's affairs with both wisdom and common sense, as his son Gerald has continued to do.

The letters in the present volume add greatly to the understanding of D. H. Lawrence, who has become, at last, what is generally known as a 'classic'.

1 Letters between Frieda Lawrence and Edward W. Titus

Beau Soleil
[Bandol,
Var,
France]

Wednesday
[5 February 1930]

Dear Titus,

I am thrilled that you are doing another 10,000 Lady C's! To-morrow I take Lawr. to a sanatorium—'Ad Astra', Vence, A. M. It's so bitter for him—I enjoyed your visit here—Isn't it maddening about Boni and L's books in America—would you ask Michael Arlen again what he thinks of Pollinger—the agent Curtis Brown haven't done anything—for years in America—I only wish I could fight, but L doesn't want me to—couldn't a firm just take those Boni books and print them? they are ours it seems to me, there's never been a contract with Boni, and [Thomas] Seltzer hasn't paid his debt—the books are out of print—many—It doesn't seem to matter who has the books, but that this priceless unique property should bring us not 200 dollars a year in America and Lawr's having sweated his guts out for this filthy humanity, that doesn't even pay him back in money not to speak of life, there he gets nothing. It makes me quite furious—the doctore (Morland) said: If he didn't go into a sanatorium, he would be dead in 3 months! But 6 years ago they told me he would be dead in a year, or two—I am so glad you haven't been on a contract—proper-business-footing with Lawr—It just takes all the life out of him—this so-called business, which is really doing each other in the eye—they do nothing but call L a degenerate,

1

nothing but insults, my goodness, they aren't worth it the canaille, and there he is ill, so ill! I shall stay here, go backwards and forwards.

Pollinger means well but is soft!

I have my lovely daughter Barby with me—hope Lawr. can stand the journey—Our lunch with you was the last 'feast' L has had and will have for some time—cheer him up if you write

You know I don't exaggerate his grievances against a foul world!

My greetings to you.
Frieda L——

Won't they say how great he is, if he were dead?

12 February 1930

Dear Mrs Lawrence:

It was a pleasure to hear from you. I wish I knew a way out of the American mess.

You say that there are no contracts, but there must have been an agreement of some sort. Had there not been, I don't for the life of me see how Curtis Brown could have allowed things to drag on the way they did.

There is just a possibility that I may be able to run down south again for a few days, as a very near relative of mine—my wife, to be explicit—is due to be there shortly. She is arriving direct from New York at Cannes the end of this month. It just depends how long she will be there and whether it will be worth my while to go down there or wait until she comes up to Paris.

You must be very happy to have your daughter with you; at least, I suppose she is still with you.

I shall long remember the little luncheon we had together—I think the three of us felt quite happy, which doesn't often happen in life, and it is precisely these little happenings that add a little zest.

I saw Michael Arlen just a day or two before your letter arrived, and I shall try to see him again so as to get his views on the matter.

I hope Mr Lawrence won't mind my writing to you on these

things. He shouldn't, of course, since we both mean it for the best.

I shall be looking forward to good news as to his condition.

Yours very sincerely,
Edward W. Titus

Mrs Frieda Lawrence
Ad Astra
Vence, A. M.

Hotel
Vence, A. M.

Saturday
[c. 15 February 1930]

Dear Mr Titus,

It was good of you to write so promptly—I fear I burst out rather fiercely at you, but I was very distressed about Lawr you see. I have to be so controlled with him—I hope you didn't mind—I feel so bitterly for him with all he has given to the world, he has had so much more meanness than he has had kindness—He minds not so much the money about Seltzer, but he was fond of him and that he let him down was a real grief to him—Poor little Seltzer let himself down—Yes, there were agreements with Seltzer and it said he must pay every 6 months, but Pollinger told me, if an editor doesn't pay that's no reason for taking your books back—there never were agreements with Boni—Rich, the Curtis Brown man in New York, hates Lawr's work. Michael Arlen knows Pollinger; perhaps he would talk to him in London—You see a bit of friendliness goes such a long way with Lawrence. Yes, it would be jolly if you could come and I hope you will have a nice time with your wife—My daughter Barbara is a godsend, she is lovely inside and out—Lawr is so sad, can't eat and doesn't gain weight, only 44.2 kili he weighs—I try hard to think of things to comfort him, but when I said yesterday, you'll see we'll have some jolly times yet, he said: that will be in heaven my dear—I don't care about heaven, but perhaps it may be alright—It's a shame to bother you and please don't take much trouble, we have some money anyhow, and you are quite busy enough—We shall be, Barby and I, at <u>Cagnes</u> <u>Casa</u>

dei Logni Place du Château—Friends have lent us it—I wish
we knew a person with a yacht, to take L for a voyage, that
might buck him up. Yes, Lawr would mind my writing to you
about business, but I don't think very profoundly and he hates
it so himself anyhow—Barby says everybody has read or is
reading Lady C in London—Lawr only got 1700 frs for the
Escaped Cock from Crosby, very little isn't it?

>   Very kind regards
>   Frieda L——

>   Villa Robermond
>   Quartier Chabert
>   Vence

>   Wednesday
>   [c. 15 March 1930]

Dear Edward Titus,
    Thank you for the 10,000—you will be sorry to hear that my
daughter Barby is also threatened with tuberculosis—in the
bone—her back must be put into plaster—but I hope she will
be cured—I am so glad you were with us at his end—His grave
and the love he left me and his greatness and the love he left to
all the world are with me—I want so much to take him to the
ranch and make a lovely place for him there—Would his
American admirers pay for his transport? There isn't much
money, as the 4000 £'s belong to his brothers and sisters, I only
get the interest for life—but with pictures and mss., I hope
they are mine, I have enough—I have written to [Witter]
Bynner to help with Boni and Seltzer—So much affection
comes in—What about the Lady C bother? Orioli comes
to-day—I am glad you are doing his letters—I think the Aga
Khan will buy his pictures—Don't tell anybody, nor about my
wanting to take him to the ranch—It's the only thing I want—

>   Yours gratefully
>   Frieda Lawrence

[Lawrence had died on 2 March.—eds]

Mme Frieda Lawrence   19 March 1930
Villa Robermond
Quartier Chabert
Vence, A. M.

Dear Mrs Lawrence:
    I have been expecting to hear from Mr [Aldous] Huxley
concerning your affairs in general, but I am without news
from him and do not know whether he is still down south, or
whether he has come back to Suresnes.
    It gave me a dreadful shock to hear of your daughter's
illness. Indeed, misfortunes never come singly. I sincerely
hope that her condition is not serious; and I have been
wondering whether it would not be better for her to go to
Berck-Plage in the north of France, which is supposed to be a
marvellous institution for this sort of trouble. I have a friend
up there, a young French writer, who seems to be progressing
very nicely. He has his entire leg, including the hip, in plaster.
    I wonder if you can let me have some details as to the legal
situation, concerning heirs, etc. Huxley promised me that he
would call on the British consul at Toulon, and let me know
the result. One really ought to know fairly definitely just what
the situation is, without letting it become complicated. Will
you be good enough to let me hear from you as soon as
possible?
    Is there any chance of your coming to Paris?
    With kindest regards, I am,

                    Yours very sincerely,
                    Edward W. Titus

                              Villa Robermond
                              Vence, A. M.

                              [c. 11 April 1930]

Dear Titus,
    Here I am back with Barby—How I miss Lawrence sleeping
in his room and thinking of him and he grows and grows for
me—How sure he was in life, how generous we were with each
other, how much he gave me, whatever I gave I got it back a
thousandfold——Now it's Eastertime and I am alone—I saw

Edward Rosenbach in London, who may give me a lot of money for the Mss; my lawyer says as Lady C is banned in England it does <u>exist</u> for the law, so you can send me the money for our beloved Lady. Have you had more bothers? I sent Aldous a list of ~~letters~~ people for letters, they are <u>wonderful</u> some of them—Do keep Aldous up to the scratch, they should come out <u>fairly</u> soon—I think—there is some more unpublished stuff of Lorenzo's tell me, what you would like, what <u>kind?</u> I saw so many people in London. What a strain! Curtis Brown are trying to play a game with me, I hate it, these inferiors! How is the Lady going, still strong, her ladyship?

My best greetings to you—Lorenzo's grave is lying so quietly in the sun with the fruit trees in bloom——

Frieda

[18 April 1930]

Dear Mrs Lawrence:

At last I have the pleasure of hearing from you. I have been wondering what happened, especially as you promised or half promised to write me from London. I had hoped to hear from you at some detail regarding the question of heirs.

What precisely is the situation and what is the definite opinion of your solicitor in London. You will understand that it is only natural for me to know the exact situation.

I will be able to let you have about 10,000 francs after the first of May. The book is still selling. I have had several inquiries regarding translation rights. If I knew just what the legal situation is, I might be able to answer. If, in your lawyer's opinion, you are now the sole owner of Lawrence's rights as an author, then we could answer the question intelligently and responsibly.

If, as far as you know, the Swedish rights have not as yet been disposed of, I would like you to tell me how much you would take for the Swedish rights of Lady C. For the French rights, I understand Lawrence accepted the sum of 1500 francs, probably plus royalties. This might perhaps serve as a criterion for the other countries, except perhaps Germany which, I believe, Lawrence had already disposed of.

Another complication seems to have arisen, and I am

examining it now, although I have not as yet reached any definite conclusion. I am afraid that pirated editions are still being sold, and I am afraid that 200 copies have been disposed of precisely in Sweden. I have not as yet the full facts before me, but I will let you know just as soon as I have my facts all together.

I am very sorry that it has been impossible for you to stop in Paris on your way back, as I would have liked to talk some things over with you. I myself cannot see my way clear to take a trip down south for quite some little while.

You tell me that you have some more unpublished stuff of Lawrence's, and you ask me what I would like: Personally, I would like almost anything if it is in finished condition, and would, in fact, like you to send me all you have. If you would let me know just what it is that you have, it would be so much easier for me to decide.

Frankly, I felt very much hurt that Orioli had been given the 'Apocalypse' before anyone knew much about it. However, the milk has been spilt, and there is no use crying. But it does seem more reasonable for you to let me have whatever there is because you can always have some money from me, even an advance; or, if there is still something more in the way of manuscripts, we might be able to do it on an equal basis, the same as Lady C., whichever you would prefer.

At all events, will you be good enough to let me know with as much detail as you can, what there is in the way of unpublished material so that I can make my choice of much or little?

Now, regarding manuscripts, which you say Rosenbach is willing to buy. I can say to you now that if you will let me know what there is in the way of manuscripts, and if you have any idea of the offer that Rosenbach is likely to make you for these same manuscripts, I myself may be able to offer you, and pay you, as much as he; and there being a choice between him and myself, I think you would only be fair to me to let me have the first refusal.

I don't know whether Mr Huxley is in town now. He left Paris some days ago, I believe, and he promised to get in touch with me upon his return. I suppose I shall hear from him shortly, but if I do not, I shall call him up.

I will be very much obliged if you will let me hear from you as soon as possible. I do hope that your daughter is better, and that I may soon have the pleasure of seeing both of you in Paris.

Yours most sincerely,
Edward W. Titus

Mrs Frieda Lawrence
Villa Robermond
Vence, A. M.

[25 April 1930]

Dear Mrs Lawrence:
    May I ask you for an answer to my letter of April 18th?

Sincerely yours,
Edward W. Titus

Mrs Frieda Lawrence
Villa Robermond
Vence, A. M.

Vence

Friday
[25 April 1930]

Dear Mr Titus,
    The situation isn't cleared yet about the will, as Murry reminded me that Lawr had made a will in Cornwall during the war—If the will turned up, all would be mine, but it hasn't turned up—then this is the situation when there's no will—a 1000£s for me, pictures, Mss mine, but copyrights after my death go to the family—but during my lifetime all the interest is mine and I can manage it also—Lady Chatterley does not exist in the eyes of the English law, so we are free there. Send me the 10,000 frs, as I spend a little more money now with Barby's Xrays and the . . . . she had made and all—
    I left London in a hurry, Barby worried me and I was so miserable in London, but everybody was only too nice to keep me.
    Yes, there is some unpublished stuff of Lawrence's, more than I thought. Don't forget, that Orioli was an old friend of

Lorenzo's and also feels he has a first right to his things. He also pays expenses and shares profits with me for the love of Lorenzo—I can't give you a proper list of unpublished Mss yet, because I don't quite know what has been published and what not—

There are, thank goodness, lots of Mss and it will amuse you to hear that I said I wanted the whole lot, or practically all, 25,000 pounds. I don't care much, what I get, but it angers me, also I know that people want them.

Aldous is in

Les Flots
Cap de la Gorge

They bought the house, it's quite near your Bandol Hotel on that foreland—he goes to in May and will surely see you.

I wish you would come down—I stay here till Barby is better. Have the house till end of September—may then go to New Mexico—Jo Davidson sent Rosenbach to me—How is your theatre going? That interests me very much—The Swedish rights for Lady C, sell them but tell Pollinger—How beastly, still pirates about.

With all good wishes
Frieda Lawrence

28 April 1930

Dear Mrs Lawrence:

I am very much obliged to you for your letter, and I suppose the best thing for me to do would be to have my London solicitor get touch with yours in London so that I might get the legal end of our business in proper order. It is quite true what you say, that the book not being recognized in England would simplify the matter of itself, as far as the rights of any possible English claimants are concerned.

This situation, however, would not necessarily apply to France. If the claim is valid here, people could make it good here. The thing is probably not at all serious and everything will turn out to your satisfaction and mine; only, you will understand that I would not like to tie myself up and have complications if I can avoid them.

I will take the further risk and send you some money, as I have said, next month when the booksellers' bills fall due.

I am sorry that your letter does not reply to my request for some material to be published in my magazine, for which of course I will pay right off the bat. I had expected you would let me know what you have in the way of stories or essays. You told me when you were here in Paris that you would get together some manuscripts which were in the possession of some young man in London, whose name escapes me. Also, if there is something longer than a story for the magazine, and that would lend itself for publication in a small format, I would like to get that too. There is no reason, no practical reason at least, why Orioli should get everything, even though he was Lawrence's friend.

On the subject of the Swedish translation, you didn't tell me how much you want me to ask. Instead, you tell me simply I should sell it and inform Pollinger. Now does that mean that I have to ask him about the price? Or will it be sufficient if I simply tell him that the sale of the Swedish rights has taken place, on your instructions, and on your behalf? Kindly answer these points.

I would be very happy indeed to be able to run down again for a day or two, but I am rather busy now and I don't know when I shall be able to take any time off.

Of course, your saying that you asked that big price for all Lawrence's manuscripts does not help me in any way. First of all, I might not want all of them. And secondly, the price you asked is amusing indeed, as you say. I don't believe that it is within the realm of practical business.

If you can name any particular manuscripts that are in your possession, and that you are willing to dispose of, name these manuscripts to me together with the prices, and I will seriously consider the advisability of purchasing them on a reasonable cash basis. I would be particularly interested, of course, in 'Lady Chatterley's Lover': I believe there are three versions of that. The most interesting one for me, from my point of view, would be the one that was published. But as I have said, let me know as fully as you can just what there is, and what you expect to get for them, and I'll take everything into most conscientious consideration.

I feel certain that your daughter's health will go on

improving gradually, and that there is a happy life in front of her.

Yours very sincerely,
Edward W. Titus

Mrs Frieda Lawrence
Villa Robermond
Vence, A. M.

Vence

Wednesday
[30 April 1930]

Dear Mr Titus,

   Percy Robinson's address is 15 Great Marlborough Street, London. Perhaps you would write to him direct and give him a short statement of facts and receipts, I also don't want to get into trouble with possible heirs and so on—My asking Rosenbach for 25,000 £ may not be practical business, but it's big, imaginative business and I know in my bones what Lorenzo's things are worth—You know it too—about Swedish rights of Lady C tell Miss Leau Watson of Curtis Brown, she does the foreign things. Let her arrange it or I shall get into a muddle—I can't give you anything to publish yet, till the will is settled, but will think about a book for you and something for your magazine—I know you couldn't be otherwise but honest with me, but doesn't it grieve you to part with the money, as it does most people? Aldous had gone to London, I still owe him 7,000 frcs, that he paid for me. So send me the 10,000 on the first as you said you would and tell me how Lady C has gone, it interests me—At the trial of Lorenzo's pictures Mr Meade, the dried, old insect of a magistrate said: 'I would destroy these pictures, as I would destroy wild beasts'. Such a compliment! think of a tiger and a dirty little magistrate. Why don't all tigers eat all magistrates? I am very busy looking after many things.

Very sincerely yours
Frieda Lawrence

6 May 1930

Dear Mrs Lawrence:

I am obliged to you for your letter of Wednesday giving me Percy Robinson's address. I immediately wrote to my solicitor, Mr Collins, to get in touch with him, and I shall probably hear from him in the course of this week. You will understand that having already had so much trouble with Lady C., I would not like to get myself into any mess on the finances of it. You will therefore be good enough to be patient for a few days longer until I have heard from Mr Collins, when I shall immediately write you and make you a payment accordingly.

Lady C. is still going pretty well, and as soon as I hear from Mr Collins we shall probably be in a position to make further arrangements.

I shall write to Miss Watson of Curtis Brown's, regarding translation rights as you have suggested.

You may rest assured that I shall guard your interests in the matter to the best of my ability, even if I had to stretch a point or more points; only it would be foolish of me to proceed blindly.

Kindly remember me to your daughter, and believe me

Very sincerely yours,
Edward W. Titus

9 May 1930

Dear Mrs Lawrence:

I am afraid we are in a mess. I enclose the letter I received this morning from my London solicitors, who have been representing me in London for the last fifteen years, and whose opinion I value greatly because it is always a cool and well considered one, hence reliable. The letter speaks for itself, and having read it I would be obliged to you if you returned it to me as I am leaving myself without a copy since I preferred to send you the original rather than a copy.

You will see from his letter that I am advised on no condition to make further payments to you, because unless it is definitely settled that you are the legal successor, I might be asked and compelled to pay over again any moneys paid to you to those who are in point of law entitled to receive them.

You gave me to understand some time ago that there was

every likelihood that the sisters and brother of the late Mr Lawrence would forego any interests they might have in the estate in your favour, with some exceptions that you mentioned to me. I was in hopes that during your visit in London you would have seen to this being done, but I have had no sort of advice from you on this subject.

The position then being as it is, I can only keep a strict accounting, as for the matter of that I kept in the lifetime of Mr Lawrence, of moneys received, and keep these moneys in readiness to be paid out to whoever may turn out to be entitled to them in due course.

I have no doubt but you will understand and appreciate my situation. That you so understand it and appreciate it, you yourself in your last letter sufficiently hinted when you said that you could not let me have anything for publication in my magazine or in book form until this legal point has been settled. Although frankly, and I must still harp on the subject, you did not see fit to wait in the case of Mr Orioli, to whom you gave one or more manuscripts for publication. I mention this not with any grudge, but simply as being quite relevant to the situation.

If you see a way whereby I can, without running any risk, make payments, I am open to any suggestion or plan that you might submit, because as I assured you before, repeatedly, I would prefer to be helpful to you, knowing you as I do, rather than to others who mean nothing to me. So please let me know fully just what I might do sensibly without putting my neck into a noose.

Yesterday, only, I met a gentleman who told me he had seen it reported in a German paper—a Frankfurt paper I believe he said—that the relatives of Mr Lawrence intend to take proceedings to suppress Lady C. Have you heard anything on the subject?

I must ask you to be as frank with me as possible in everything concerning this affair, because it is only by mutual frankness that we will be best able to serve each other. I don't know of anyone with whom I could freely discuss this matter except you and Mr Huxley. I should like to see Mr Huxley as soon as possible, but I understand he is still in London. He, knowing the situation perfectly well, might be helpful to us both in solving the knot. I wonder whether you would not suggest to him, if you know his London address, to come in to see me as soon as he gets back from London, so that a conclusion of some sort might be reached to your satisfaction.

Yours very sincerely,
Edward W. Titus

Mrs D. H. Lawrence
Villa Robermond
Vence, A. M.

E. W. Titus Esq,   Wild, Collins & Crosse
4 Rue Delambre,   Solicitors
Paris xiv,   Kennan's House,
France   Crown Court,
                                        behind No. 65, Cheapside,
                                              London E. C. 2.

7 May 1930

Dear Mr Titus,

I have your letter of the 5th instant, and I will, if necessary, arrange to see Mr Robinson, but before I do so, I would like to reply to your letter.

The only people whom you are entitled to deal with, and who can give a valid receipt for any money paid, would be the executors or administrators of the late Mr D. H. Lawrence.

So far as our law is concerned, the question of the administration of the estate would depend on the domicile of Mr Lawrence. The mere fact that he lived in France or what was his nationality, would not affect the question. The point is, whether he intended to live in France perpetually, or intended to return to England, that is to say, whether he retained his British domicile, or whether he had acquired a French domicile.

This is a question of fact, to be proved by evidence. If he still remained a domiciled Englishman, although resident abroad, then our Courts would have to grant the Letters of Administration or prove the Will, and in this case the British Authorities would claim estate duty on his personal estate, and would administer the estate in accordance with English law.

If, on the other hand, he had acquired a French domicile, then the administration of the estate would be in the hands of the French Authorities and duty on the property in France would be payable to the French Authorities.

It might be if he had a British domicile, duties would be payable in France on property situate within the jurisdiction of that country, but the law relating to the division of his property would entirely depend on whether he were domiciled in England or in France.

At any rate, you ought not to deal with Mrs Lawrence, but only with an official administrator by whatever country he may be appointed.

It is for the Courts of the Country to decide who are the persons entitled to administer the estate. If Lawrence made a will and it has not been revoked, this should be proved. Even if it cannot be found, our Courts would prove it, on being satisfied that it had really only been lost, and whatever were the contents.

I do not think you ought to pay Mrs Lawrence any money, because if there were a contract between you and the late Mr Lawrence, it might be that an executor or administrator will be constituted, who could recover from you, any money you had improperly paid to the widow.

I do not think there is anything in the point of the book having been banned in England. It was not banned in France, and it was perfectly open for Mr Lawrence to make arrangements with you, for the publication of the book in France, and any contract he had made with you, would be, I think, enforced by our Courts. This is a principle of contract which has been decided in this country, that a contract made abroad, about a matter which would be illegal in this country, is enforceable and can be sued on.

If you were in England, I should advise you to carry any royalties payable to Mr Lawrence, to a separate account, and wait until you receive an application from an official executor or administrator. I think you would be safe in dealing with an administrator appointed by the French Courts. Indeed, even if Probate were granted in this country, or if Letters of Administration were granted here, you, as a resident in France, would be entitled to say, it must be proved by the Authorities in France, before you would pay over the money.

I do not see any advantage of my seeing Mr Percy Robinson

at present, and I will wait to hear from you in reply to this letter, before making an appointment with him.

Yours sincerely,
Algernon L. Collins

Vence

[c. 11 May 1930]

Dear Mr Titus,

In reply to your letter of May the 9th, as far as I am concerned there is no mess. The situation is now quite clear. You are accountable to the estate for the royalties, and as soon as letters of administration have been granted, which will be in a few days, you will be told whom to pay.

I have made no arrangements with Mr Orioli other than those made by Lawrence before his death, namely for the publication of the 'Virgin and the Gipsy'. Lawrence left a good many Mss in his care and Mr Orioli is retaining them on behalf of the estate. He has been instructed not to proceed with the publication of any of the other Mss until letters of administration have been granted,

So that's that,

Sincerely yours
Frieda Lawrence

Kingsley Hotel
Hart Street
[London]

Friday
[c. 25 July 1930]

Dear Mr Titus,

Next week I come to Paris, don't know yet when I can get off—I'll come and see you, or hear the news—Orioli has just been called on by the enemy—I hear in Vence and all sorts of places her Ladyship is much in request—I shall have a letter of administration and all that, so that you can give me my share—Better not draw too much attention, the lawyer and I agreed—

Yours sincerely,
Frieda Lawrence

I'll bring you a photograph of the grave with the phoenix on it——

Mrs Frieda Lawrence   28 July 1930
Kingsley Hotel
Hart Street, London

Dear Mrs Lawrence:

It has been an age since I heard from you. I ~~am~~ was, in fact, on the point of trying to reach Aldous Huxley, to gain information as to the legal status of ~~affairs~~ the case.

I am very anxious to have the matter cleared up. I ~~only~~ expect that I shall be in Paris when you come through, as otherwise I would have to ask you to please provide myself with a copy of the certificate of appointment as administrator, which you would be good enough to leave with my secretary when you are here during my absence. I would then immediately make out a statement and send it to the address which you would be good enough to leave.

I was very much hurt having no news from you of any sort for such a long spell. You have left me at sea completely as to what was going on, and I found it naturally very embarrassing for quite a number of reasons, despite the fact that you wrote me some time back that Orioli had held up the publication of his book until the settlement of the administration. He wrote to me quite some time ago, when I ordered a couple of copies from him, that the book was completely sold out. It was advertised, as you know, quite some ~~time~~ months ago.

And I am also still waiting for some promised material for publication. Everybody in London has had new Lawrence stuff published, but myself.

Very sincerely yours
Edward W. Titus

Kingsley Hotel
Hart Street
London

Tuesday
[? 5 August 1930]

Dear Mr Titus,

Yes, now I think it's a long time since I wrote—but I had no definite news—George Lawrence and I are co-administrators but all royalties are mine, and later on will come direct to me, only at present it needs both George's and my signature—I will talk to Mr Pollinger how best to get your money, because we don't officially want to draw attention to Lady C—I feel in Italy it's the money made, they begrudge—the German Lady C is beautifully translated and sells well—already first 4500 sold—Nobody had anything of Lawrence's, that they didn't have before his death; again I'll talk to Pollinger, what we can send you—the lawyer seems quite helpless as to Lady C; the poor Lady floats in the air, legally anyhow; as far as England is concerned non-existent, I'll let you know definitely what to do—

Yours very sincerely
Frieda Lawrence

I detest it all this business—could you tell me, where George Seldes is?

Villa Robermond
Vence

12 Aug 1930

Dear Mr Titus,

I know it will grieve you to hear, that I have been through some more great sorrow. My lovely Barby has been so ill, quite off her head, these last 3 weeks—It has been so terrible—I can't tell you. I can't get on top of it—But she is better now, but weak—I have every hope to pull her through, but it will be a long job. Pollinger says, it will be quite all right, if you send me some money; I am spending a lot with her illness as you can imagine. My other daughter, Elsa is here, she is married; we have a sad time, they were so fond of each other. To see those two beautiful creatures together, is sad, I can tell you—

Orioli had some more trouble with Lady C—Who is the blighter in England who is so 'pure'? How is the theatre? I was so thrilled by it—If you see Arabella, please tell her, that just as she wanted me to see her in Nice, Barby was very bad —

Yours very sincerely and sadly
Frieda Lawrence

15 Sep 1930

My dear Mrs Lawrence,
The postman has just brought me your letter and I hastened to enclose a cheque for Frcs. 5000.oo. Technically and legally speaking I should not do this as you know, but I just cannot let you write me such a letter and not respond to it in a practical manner.—I have heard from Lawrence's brother and written to him. I also wrote to my London solicitor to get in touch with him and have him draw up the letter which I hope will straighten out the matter for us so that we can run along smoothly. The book is still selling pretty well, but with the tourist season soon coming to an end, sales will doubtless slow down.
I spent a fortnight in Italy, at Forte di Marmi, which you well know, and went up to Florence for one day hoping to be able to see ~~him~~ Orioli, but found his shop closed; so could not see him, which I much regretted.
What has happened with the Lawrence letters with reference to which Aldous Huxley made me a definite promise? I have not heard from him for ever so long. Would you not be good enough to ask him for me? I have not his present address.—I saw Arabella since her return from the South and I was 'wie zerschmettert' when she told me of your new dreadful trouble. If I have two or three days to spare, I shall run up to see you and tell you how really and truly sorry I am to hear of how cruelly fate is trying you.

Yours very sincerely,
Edward W. Titus

Villa Robermond
Vence, A. M.

Wednesday
[c. September 1930]

Dear Mr Titus,

You are a real friend indeed—I mean at the moment I just am short of money—There is so much to do with my poor Barby and it's almost too much that's on my shoulders—Thank you so very much for your prompt and practical help—I have just written to my sister-in-law Ada (she is quite for me) to make the other two sign a paper, that all they want is the copyrights after my death, that would simplify things. Orioli will come in October, perhaps you can come when he is here, I will try and arrange it—I will also write to Aldous, I told Pollinger about the promise Aldous and I gave you about the letters—they are being collected—I am taking another house, because Barby suffered so much here, my grief and her own—One day she ran out past that room were Lawrence died and cried in such a terrible voice: 'There's nothing, nothing, nothing anymore.' And another time: 'My poor mother her child is dead'—I can tell you the bottomless pit I know if there are things worse than death—that poor child, she is such an exceptional creature really and so amusing— Well, there it is—I never wanted an easy life, but this was more than one can stand—Anyhow many thanks for your quick help—I have about 500 £s in England, still hope they won't melt too quickly in this disaster. So don't worry about my money, please—your theatre thrills me, something jolly being done somewhere anyhow—I found some wonderful letters of Lawr to me, the first 14—all I have—

Ever yours,
Frieda Lawrence

Greet Arabella from me—

Mrs F. Lawrence,   9 October [? 1930]
Villa Robermond,
Vence, A. M.

Dear Mrs Lawrence,
    Just a line to let you know that I now have the letter from Mr
George Lawrence authorising me to deal with you directly.
My book keeper is ill for the moment and as soon as she gets
back to work I shall take up the matter of the account. In the
meantime, however, if you wish to have some money let me
know.
    While I am writing to you may I mention that a London
friend of mine wrote to me asking me to get him a copy of the
Apocalypse which he tells me Orioli—the lucky and favoured
Orioli—is to bring out shortly, if he has not done so as yet.
    Perhaps if you have a chance and write to Orioli you might
ask him to reserve two copies for me.
    I hope your troubles are not as acute now as they were some
time back, and remain,

                    Yours very sincerely,
                    Edward W. Titus

Mrs F. Lawrence,   22 October 1930
Villa Robermond,
Vence, A. M.

Dear Mrs Lawrence,
    I am obliged to leave for Vienna for about ten days and I
thought it might be welcome to you to receive some money
from me in the interim. I am obliged to go away before the
statement of the account has been quite completed. Mrs Titus,
who had gone to Vienna, was taken ill suddenly and had to be
operated upon for appendicitis. She is quite all right now and
I am going to bring her back to Paris. On my return you will
hear from me again. In the meantime I enclose a cheque for
Frs. 10,000.
    I wrote to you some time back asking you to be kind enough
to order me two copies of the 'Apocalypse' from Orioli. I hope

it was not too much trouble for you to do this.

In case you should like to write to me in the next few days a letter addressed to me at the Hotel Imperial, Vienna, Austria, will reach me or will be forwarded.

With kindest greetings,

Yours very sincerely,
Edward W. Titus

Mrs Frieda Lawrence,   1 December 1930
Les Aspras,
Route de Coursegoules,
Vence, A. M.

Dear Mrs Lawrence,

I hope you will get this letter because the new address that you have given me is not very legible and I am just guessing at it. I am giving you the following statement of account for 6,000 copies of 'Lady Chatterley's Lover':

2,266 copies at Frs. 34 net	Frs.	76,672
2,600 copies at " 36 net		93,000
1,145 copies at " 40 net		45,800
	Frs.	216,072

Expenditure—6,000 copies at Frs. 4.55 ...Frs. 27,306
Income Tax & Chiffre d'affaires 10% .... "   21,607.20
                                Frs. 48,913.20 Frs. 48,913.20
                                              Frs. 167,158.80

Lawrence's Share 8/15ths ....Frs. 89,151.36
Titus's Share   7/15ths................ "   78,007.44
                                     Frs. 167,158.80
                                     Frs. 89,151.36

Lawrence's Share Paid 27/2/30 Frs. 10,000
      "   15/9/30   5,000
      "   22/10/30   10,000
Advocate's charges incidental in connec- Frs. 25,000
tion with prosecution—Frs. 8,000—half of   64,151.36
which   "   4,000
                                  Frs. 60,151.36

On account of above I enclose cheque for Frs. 20,000, the balance of which will be paid you as more money is collected.

I am ordering 5,000 more copies to be printed and I would like to have your formal assent to that as well as an acknowledgement of the receipt of the present cheque.

I have been asked to approach you by a very prominent publisher in London in connection with the publication of 'Apocalypse'. I have undertaken to write to you on the subject with the understanding that there is no compensation to be made to me from any side if the deal goes through. I think the proposition is probably the best that was ever made to D.H. in his lifetime and it would be a very foolish thing not to accept it. You should lose no time in writing to your brother-in-law to get him to accept it no matter what Curtis Brown might have to say about it. I feel that the estate is free to act in this matter since the book is not a novel and as I understand the Agreement with Secker includes novels only, or probably also poetry, but the Apocalypse is not poetry either, of course. If Secker or anyone else through Curtis Brown would make a similar proposition hesitation in accepting it might be justified, but only hesitation, because I doubt whether any other firm except the one that I have in mind would push the book with the same energy.

Briefly, I am authorised to offer you £5,000 advance royalties immediately on the agreement being entered into and and royalties to be on the basis of 15% going up to 25%.

I think I will be safe in betting that no such agreement has ever been made to your late husband, or to his estate since his death. I want to have your views on the subject as soon as possible, and when your agreement has been obtained the London firm will take up the matter with your brother-in-law.

Another thing that ought to be considered is that the manner in which the book would be put before the public by the firm interested in it must also have an advantageous effect on Lawrence's other books and should surely help to increase their sales.

Yours very sincerely,
Edward W. Titus

'Les Aspras'
Vence, A. M.

Friday
[? 5 December 1930]

Dear Mr Titus,

You seem to know by instinct or the Lord tells you, when I am running short of money. Thank you for the cheque. The arrangement with Lawrence and you about our Lady is so frightfully decent, on your part.

Since I wrote to you I have been to Baden-Baden, where my good, my dear mother died—Barby went to London with a nurse the day I left for Baden—I came too late to see her, my mother, Fate is cruel to me this year and Barby's awful illness had quite got me under and now this. I am really sick of misery. Perhaps now it's finished. But it was so awful to come to the door and be told: 'Die Frau Baronin ist seit——tot.'

Yes, of course print the other 5,000 Lady C's—About the Apocalypse it is indeed a noble offer but I had promised Orioli an edition of 800, I'll ask him at once what he says. He is in great trouble about Lady C and 'Gastione' another book— the man in Paris, who is translating Lady C is coming to see me—I'll also tell George about the offer. I just think the Apocalypse is mine, Lawrence gave it me, and said, 'look through it and see what you think of it and alter what you think', but I wouldn't dare touch it. He died before he could go over it again. I am very busy, found the first 14 letters of Lawrence to me, wonderful ones, all I have—Now I sit all alone in my villa and try to recover my wits, and my spirit—

Yours very sincerely
Frieda Lawrence

Mrs Frieda Lawrence,   9 December 1930
Les Aspras,
Vence, A. M.

Dear Mrs Lawrence,

I have your letter of last Friday. I am glad you are pleased with my activity. I, for my own part, am not so very pleased with the way things are going and I would very much like to talk them over with you. I would like to know what your movements are going to be for that reason. I hope to go down south for a few days to join my family who will be spending Christmas and New Year holidays somewhere South. My two boys will leave College in a day or two and I have to give them some sort of a holiday. When down South I would like to call on you.

When I hint at dissatisfaction on my part it is not on account of Lady C. but on account of feeling grieved at not being treated as I feel I should be. It was clearly understood at the time when I took over the publication of that book, that it was not that book that I was chiefly interested in. The risk I had to run to publish it could not be compensated by any amount of money I could possibly be making publishing it. That did not interest me and I made my point perfectly clear. It was a longer view that I took, which was that I counted on publishing other things of Lawrence. It was that prospect that interested me chiefly. Unfortunately, not only for me, but for the world, Lawrence was not in a position to fulfil his promise to let me have something else. After his death you renewed the promise. And when Orioli published the Gypsy story and I mentioned it to you you said you had promised it to him and could not very well not keep the promise. That is good enough as far as it goes, but one promise should be as good as another. I cannot see on what grounds the promises made to Orioli should have greater sanctity than promises made to Titus. I quite lately called your attention also, to the absolute silence of Aldous Huxley in connection with the publication of letters to be edited by him. That was also a promise but so far I am kept in the dark.

Now again, the question of the 'Apocalypse' comes up and this again has been given to Orioli although in this instance you say the 'Apocalypse' is yours. You mentioned the book 'Gaston' but you did not say whether that was also a Lawrence book. If it is not, then I have nothing to say in the matter, but if it is, I feel that insult is added to injury.

The offer I have been authorised to make to you of Five Hundred Pounds for 'Apocalypse' has nothing to do with my grievance and it is a thing quite apart from anything I say in this letter. It only shows to me that, charming and delightful a man as Orioli is, by having tied yourself up with him with this particular book you stand in your own light and work to your own disadvantage. That is all I have to say on the point. I must find out whether the publication of 'Apocalypse' in the limited edition of such a great number as eight hundred copies will not impair the proposal made to me by the London house. There is just a possibility that it may not, but in any case I would of course have to disclose this fact to the London publisher and if he does not mind, so much the better. In any event, I shall not write to him till I have heard from you after Orioli has written to you on the subject. You will please let me know as soon as you have heard from him.

Kindly let me know also, whether you propose to remain at Vence the next fortnight or so, so that I may know whether I shall be able to see you when I am in the neighbourhood.

Accept, please, my sincere sympathy in the loss of your mother. You have indeed had your share of trouble lately and I sincerely hope that the new year may make things smoother for you.

Yours very sincerely,
Edward W. Titus

Vence

Friday
[? 12 December 1930]

Dear Mr Titus,

Yes, do come and see me and I have some 'Lawrence' for you, I hope, very interesting—Bring your boys too, won't you? I may be going away from the 20th to the 28th, or the 30th; Lawrence's sister Ada (she is the nice one), will come to stay with me—

So take your choice before the 20 or after the 28th—

Yours in haste
Frieda Lawrence

Mrs Frieda Lawrence,   7 January 1931
Les Aspras,
Vence, A. M.

Dear Mrs Lawrence,

I have read with deep interest the manuscript on Hardy you confided to me the other day during my only too short call at your house. It is an amazing piece of work, although, as you say, it has little to do with Hardy and is Lawrence all over. Frankly stated, however, I should not care to publish it because it does not at all fit into the frame of what I propose to do within the near future. If I may venture an opinion, this manuscript should not be published except in connection with Lawrence's collected works whenever the time may come for their publication. It embraces, as far as I can see, the whole of Lawrence's philosophy and should be read really only after all his other books have been read, although it seems to have been written much earlier than the series of his later books.

There are however two or three chapters in the manuscript which I would like to use in my magazine. The chapters I have in mind are sufficiently self-contained to be suitable for 'This Quarter'. If you are agreeable and can tell me how much I would have to pay you for, say, two chapters, and after we have agreed upon the sum, I will have these chapters copied out of the manuscript and return to you the latter.

I am enclosing the promised draft of the note to Messrs Albert and Charles Boni. If you send it off as it is or modify it to your liking and hear from them in reply, I shall be very happy to know the result.

On re-reading this letter I find that I have perhaps not made myself clear on the subject of a Lawrence manuscript for publication as soon as I can get one. I still ask you to see whether there is amongst the material left behind some manuscript that would better fit in with my requirements. I would particularly like a longish story. I recall, of course, your mentioning the 'Escaped Cock'. This would have suited me first rate as an unpublished work, but I never publish reprints. The only exception I made in this policy was in the case of 'Lady Chatterley's Lover' and even then I made it my first condition that new matter be added to it as indeed it had been in the introduction. If there are other manuscripts available I should gladly examine them if you give me the opportunity. If there are none, I shall indeed by very unhappy over it and feel that I have not been as fairly dealt with as I had hoped to be.

Yours very sincerely,
Edward W. Titus

Vence

Saturday
[? 10 January 1931]

Dear Mr Titus,

It was nice of you to take all that trouble—I have sent the letter to them, putting it a bit more in my own language—This is to say, that I shall be in ~~Lon~~ Paris on the 15th in the evening at the Versailles, Orioli is coming with us—So you'll see him too—I hate going to London, but must—Yours was a short visit—But thank you ever so much—There may be a short story or two in the American Mss—About those chapters we must ask Frere Reeves I suppose—

Very sincerely
Frieda Lawrence

Kingsley Hotel
Hart Street
London

Sunday
[? 18 January 1931]

Dear Mr Titus,

We are trying to get on with all the jobs—Frere Reeves and Orioli—I want to tell you quickly that that pirated edition of <u>our</u> Lady you sent me with the photograph of Davidson's bust in it was done <u>here</u>—We know by whom; Orioli is <u>so</u> angry that on the first page it says 'Printed in Florence etc'—We just found out this minute—We can stop them though—I won't take any money for it, but only stop them—What a lot of fighting one has to do—O Lord—To-morrow night I dine with Michael Arlen—So send Reeves the Thomas Hardy—

Kindest regards
Frieda Lawrence

Mrs Frieda Lawrence,   20 January 1931
Kingsley Hotel,
Hart Street,
London

Dear Mrs Lawrence,
    I am sending the Hardy manuscript to Mr. Frere Reeves direct as you want me to do. You remember I thought there would be two chapters in the book that I would like to use in the magazine and pay for it, of course. Inasmuch as you are apparently in a hurry for me to hand the book to Frere Reeves, I have not had time to choose the chapters I would like best for publication, and would ask you, if Frere Reeves takes the book, to let me have the manuscript again for not more than a day or so so that I might choose the portion suitable.
    I note what you say regarding the pirated English edition. I do not for one moment believe that you will countenance that enterprise by taking hush money. On the other hand I am very pessimistic as to whether you can do anything to stop the book, although you seem to think you can. I, personally, believe that it is best to let things alone.
    I am holding you to your promise to stop at Paris on your return trip.

                  Yours very sincerely,
                  Edward W. Titus

Mrs Frieda Lawrence,   4 April 1931
Les Aspras,
Vence

Dear Mrs Lawrence,
    Not having heard from you for a long time I am wondering whether you are still at the same address. I should be glad if you would write and assure me as I have some money to send you.

                  Yours very sincerely,
                  Edward W. Titus

Vence

[9 April 1931]

Dear Mr Titus,

Thank you for your letter—I hoped you would turn up before now—I have an exhibition here and it's a great success—the pictures look much nicer than in London in a simple place—I have a letter of Lawrence's for you, you know, the simple agreement you had with him—I am very busy—Do send me as much money as you can, I must go to America—I have <u>not</u> received (not at all) all that due to me and still fighting for Mss—What a life!

Sincerely yours,
Frieda Lawrence

Mrs Frieda Lawrence,   29 April 1931
Les Aspras,
Vence, A.M.

Dear Mrs Lawrence,

I am enclosing a cheque for Frs. 10,000 and you will be good enough to acknowledge receipt. I would like to be kept au courant as to the date of your going to America as well as to your movements there and the approximate time of your return. If business picks up one must keep in view the possibility of further printing and I would like to have you and myself be prepared for it.

Yours very sincerely.
Edward W. Titus

Vence, A. M.

Friday
1 May 1931

Dear Mr Titus,

Here's the cheque for 10,000 frcs—you'll send me more soon, won't you? At the ranch? Kiowa Ranch, Taos, New Mexico—I am keen to go, but it hurts me too to leave Lawrence here—I am not taking him as it said in the papers—<u>Contradict</u> <u>it</u> for me, will you? Can't you do anything about Lady C being sold in England? I'll try once more—If you come to America, come to the ranch—I wonder how I shall find it—How we loved it there! I can't still believe he is dead! And he grows and grows, for other people too—Aren't you glad you met him, though it was when he was ill? It seems all a dream, that life with him and I see him as such a wonderful thing, only a radiance in spite of all temper and difficulties! It's too much to know, what he was I always knew it a bit, when [?] not so completely! How is the theatre? Do tell me—I am thinking of Lawrence on your stage, but the thing itself [?] me so much!

Kindest regards,
Frieda

I am leaving here <u>Monday</u>

Les Aspras
Route de Coursegoules
Vence, A. M.

[? early May 1931]

Dear Mr Titus,
    It was good of you to send me those 10,000! I am sorry Mrs Titus has been ill. What a worry for you. My daughter is much better, is going to get quite well, it will take some time yet, but it is a pleasure looking after her, she is such a dear! I don't hear from Orioli, I fear he is ill—I am sure the 'Apocalypse' is by no means ready—He and Douglas came to see me in Baden-Baden, but I haven't heard much since—Brother-in-law, George is a slippery proposition, I fear, I would so like to be his enemy! I fear their libations are too copious! As he is Lawrence's in spirit, really! Things in America seem hopeless too, there's an unauthorised, abridged edition of Lady C—I am sorry you can't come back this way with Mrs Titus to see me, I wish you could—

So many thanks
Yours very sincerely
Frieda Lawrence

Vence

Thursday
[? early May 1931]

Dear Mr Titus,

I wrote to you to-day, now I am writing again—My sister brought me 3 plays of Lawrence's, he had left them at her place in the 'Isartal' years ago. One I love very much, it's when we were first together, Now I wonder if you would have them typed for me quickly before I go to America. I am a bit scared of these Mss—I would send them registered, If it's not too much bother for you, send me a telegram and I'll send them at once—

Sincerely yours
Frieda Lawrence

It is such <u>lovely</u> weather!
Say just 'oui' in the telegram—And send about 20 Lady C's, people are asking for them at the exhibition—

Vence

20 [May] 1931

Dear Mr Titus,

Thank you for the telegram—No, I am not sending the plays after all, I found somebody here—One play I'll take with me to put into my own book—~~Send a dozen Lady C's people ask for them at the exhibition~~ I want to get away, I am just worked too hard and I hate it—I and business! Never was anybody more unfit for it! And I come ~~him~~ in for Lawrence's 'glory' and I don't know what to do with it! He has escaped that anyhow! What about your theatre? Send me the money soon—I just met an elegant young man from Hollywood, saying I have sold enough Lady C's to keep you for a year—And not a sou for me—O dear!

Yours, like a fish, who has to take to another element,
Frieda Lawrence

Think, Lady C's are already here! I wish you were in New York to help me—I am scared.

Kiowa Ranch
Taos
New Mexico

15 July 1931

Dear Mr Titus,

Well, here I am and so glad to be here—It is a wonderful place and I hope one day you will come and see me here—I had a hard time and an exciting one in New York, now I think there'll be a law-suit to get the books away from Boni & Seltzer—I saw a man called [Samuel] <u>Roth,</u> who has done a Lady C edition. But he was an awful man—He did a play of Lady C so terrible that I can't take his money—So here I am—And the lawyer won't give me the royalties and I had been promised them—It's an awful fight and I feel swindled all the time—If you can send me some money, I shall be glad—I bought a car here and I had some expenses on the ranch and all the people, that we knew are so glad to have me back and I feel at home—in this big, free world—not so tight as Europe, all my fight is coming back into me—How are you? I don't know anything <u>definite</u> about the letters, I am not told much until I get nasty—Lady C must have made <u>lots</u> and lots of money, but alas none for me—

Yours ever
Frieda Lawrence

Mrs Frieda Lawrence,   12 August 1931
Kiowa Ranch,
Taos,
New Mexico,
U.S.A.

Dear Mrs Lawrence,

I am glad to have received your letter of the 18th [15th ?] ultimo giving me your American address. A certain development has taken place which makes it necessary for me to write to you. The sales of Lady C. have considerably fallen off, but that perhaps is to be expected as the book is no longer at its prime. The falling off is not perhaps due to that alone. News has reached me two pirated editions of the book had appeared in England, from one of which at least I am told from what must be a reliable source that you had received money, through an intermediary whose name I need not mention. That I am afraid is not cricket. Every time a pirated edition of the book appears our joint enterprise suffers. Such being the case I shall have to give up my interest in this joint enterprise.

As you seem to be in need of money I enclose my cheque for Francs: 10,000. Final settlement will under the circumstances not take place until your return to Europe. I feel that I have not at all been fairly treated by you in this matter.

Yours very sincerely,
Edward W. Titus

Kiowa Ranch
Taos
New Mexico

2 September 1931

Dear Mr Titus,

Thank you for the 10,000 frcs—Now look, I am cross that you believed I had some money from pirates in England—I didn't—I know one is Lahr or somebody with him—the second I don't know—who it can be. But I saw a terrible man called Roth at C. Brown's office, he was willing to pay me a 1,000£'s. He had also written a play on Lady C, it was so awful like himself—that I said to C. Brown (Everitt, I cannot take this man's money). I was sad about the money, but I couldn't take it—George Lawrence is a calamity, Lawrence's brother, also just refuses to pay me the royalties, or any interest from the estate, he just wants to swell the estate, it's all so low—And there I am—The Boni–Seltzer mess also gaily goes on—If it weren't that I forget it all mostly here in this wild place—I don't know where I'd be with rage—Think of the money that is made—Can't you do anything about the pirate editions—Who is the intermediary whose name you won't mention?—Whoever told you is a liar, so there! I hope you'll feel sorry you accused me of this, I had told you I wouldn't take any money from Lahr—

Yours ever,
Frieda L——

Vence
c/o Mrs Gordon Crotch
Place du Peyra

[c. 9 April 1932]

Dear Mr Titus,
    You have never given me a sign—Why? Do you believe <u>still</u>
that I took the money for Lady C, the pirated one? Are you
cross about anything? I wouldn't really care, except that you
were so decent to Lawrence and when I think you were at his
funeral I write to you—If you have a grievance, say so—I
know you are an honest man and are not merely trying to get
out of paying me the money you owe me—So what is it?
People accuse me of being greedy, I suppose, for the
expurgated Lady C, I should have thought my life has proved
the contrary—What is the book about Lawrence with the Lady
C letter in it, that I gave you? Won't you send me one and write
to me—Something had to be done to stop those pirates—How
is the theatre? Aldous has written a short, and what he read to
me, charming introduction to Lawrence's letters—It will be a
<u>great</u> book—

Sincerely yours
Frieda Lawrence

[? 1932]

Dear Mr Titus—
    I haven't put this together yet, but it will give you a
glimpse—I am glad we 'had it out' a bit, it always clears the
air—I can't <u>defend</u> anything I have done, what I have done
wrong, I have done it, and <u>what</u> I have done right is also
there—And I am not going to lie about it—But I <u>am</u> mad
about Enid Hilton—If she isn't honest about money, then
nobody is—If you <u>knew</u> all the stories they tell about me and
Lawrence! One just mustn't care!

Very sincerely yours,
Frieda L——

Friday [? 1932]

Dear Mr Titus,

I am sure—dead sure Enid Hilton didn't either. I bet Roth says I took his money!, but there I have witnesses that I refused it!

I also think those letters are the most genuine ever written by a man to a woman—I was wondering if you'd like to use some of these unpublished poems and letters for your paper—Or is somebody going to pounce on me? Some to my mother for instance? But perhaps you will wait a month or two till this will business is over—

Don't give up the theatre—you mustn't—I have 3 unpublished Lawrence plays!! There's a scheme on, I forgot to tell you—to turn the Vence chateau into a Lawrence Memorium theatre, money practically promised (though I shan't believe in it, till I see it—the money)—(But it's a secret still!) Anyhow some people are very keen—There's your theatre all ready, couldn't we arrange something? What do you say? Let me know—I am off Sunday morning and wish me luck and send me some money, when you can—It would be absolutely rotten if your theatre didn't materialise. I mean in itself—No personal reason.

I hope your wife will go on getting better and I'll let you know, if the will comes off—Tell those people, who told you about my taking the money, that I say it's a lie, please tell them, that I am very angry about it—I wonder if Lahr or whoever published it, started the lie—Lahr has got an awful wife and he drinks too—I don't think he was a rotten to begin with but is now, I fear—I'll go and see him and I'll put a chapter in my book about the money part and Lawrence's work.

Very sincerely,
F L

Kingsley Hotel
Hart Street
London WC1

Monday [? 1932]

Dear Mr Titus,

I will come and see you; here I am fighting my fight and there's a chance of fighting it successfully to the end. I hope you are convinced I never took any money for Lady C over here nor alas in America could I take it from the awful man Roth, he was too awful, one could <u>not</u> take his money. You see apart from you, if I took the money for Lady C here, I could be put in prison also the book bears Pino's [Orioli's] Florence press address—I would not do it for <u>his</u> sake—But in Florence they told me, that they were selling your Lady C—I hope this is right and I hope you can give me some more money, you owe me—How is the theatre? I have not heard—And how are you?

Sincerely yours
Frieda Lawrence

Had a good time at Florence, with Pino and Norman Douglas, who said he was writing 'love letters to a lizard' and Richard Aldington and the rest—Saw Aldous too, the D.H.L. letters are coming out before long, they will be a very great thing—

2   Letters between Frieda Lawrence and Caresse Crosby

Villa Beau Soleil
Bandol
Var

20 September 1929

Dear Harry and Caresse,

I think with such joy of my gramophone—but Orioli said, he had it in Florence, so how can it be travelling to you? I fear our new little villa will be small, but I'll take the gramophone on the rocks by the sea and shall rejoice in it all on my lonelie! Thank you very much for it! Lawrence has been ill, but now he is again getting better quickly—I think the Escaped Cock will be a dream of perfection!—Do send us your book, Caresse, we shall both be interested! You do accomplish a lot, it's amazing.

I hope you'll come and see us here sometime—The sea is so warm and the bathing so wonderful to make one yell with joy! Lorenzo is mostly cross, but I hope the sun will drive it out of him—Thank you very much for my wandering gramophone, I boast with it and I hope it will arrive—London was great fun with the fuss over L's pictures, they can't have it all their own way! I wonder how the poor bird will fare?

Many greetings from the proud possessor of the gramophone
Frieda

Beau Soleil
Bandol
Var

[November 1929?]

Dear Caresse,

I must just tell you how deeply distressed we were over Harry's death and how very, very sorry I feel for you and with you—I can't forget it and think of the days we spent with you at the mill, it's all so vivid—I am glad you have your children and you are young, but it's all so awful—

My love and sympathy
Frieda Lawrence

Villa Robermond
Vence, A. M.

[early 1930?]

Dear Caresse,

I do hope you are better—I came to see you in Paris and you were in London—No wonder you were ill—I rang you up in London and couldn't get at you, then was so busy—Now I am back again and O dear how I miss Lorenzo, in spite of illness and all, his generosity and the life he gave me—I would have loved to have seen you and talked to you, I loved Harry too—When you have time send me the 'escaped cock' and the little drawings, it was the last thing he did—If you want some other unpublished thing of his, let me know—Hoping to see you some day—Barby my daughter is with me, she also has a slight touch of TB, in the bone, isn't it too much—She is such a lovely creature—

My love to you
Frieda

Mrs D. H. Lawrence,   26 May 1930
Villa Robermond,
Vence

Dear Frieda:—

Your last letter about the manuscript of 'THE ESCAPED COCK'
has troubled me for some time, because I was sure that
Lawrence had given the manuscript to Harry before his
death, as he did the manuscript of the 'SUN', and I have found,
in looking over his letters, a letter to Harry, in which he says
that he is sending him the manuscript as a present, because he
feels he should have it, being the first one to have brought it
out. As I told you, Harry took it to New York with him and I
have not got it here in Paris. I enclose the little watercolor
motifs, which you asked for.

I am wondering if you are coming through Paris this
Spring. I should so like to see you and, as you know, I am
awfully anxious to do another one of Lawrence's unpublished
stories any time you feel like giving me something.

I love the photograph you sent me. I have a nice one,
enlarged from a snapshot, taken here at the Mill, which I am
having copied for you and will send you soon.

With ever so many good wishes and most sympathetic
thoughts.

Affectionately,
Caresse

Villa Robermond
Vence

[6 June 1930]

Dear Caresse,

How can you say Lawrence gave the Ms of the Escaped Cock
to Harry, or 'Sun'—For Sun Harry asked and paid him most
handsomely for it—I know Lawrence wanted the 'Escaped
Cock' back in Bandol—Are you only a business woman? With
the usual tricks? No, my dear, Harry was different, he wasn't
that kind—No! I won't give you another word of Lawrence's
to print if I don't get the Ms of the Escaped Cock.

Yours in disgust,
Frieda

Mrs D. H. Lawrence,   26 June 1930
Villa Robermond,
Vence.

My dear Frieda

I do not like to think the last letter I received was really written by you. I was so amazed that I am sure there must be some mistake.

I can only repeat what I wrote to you last that Lawrence I know gave Harry the manuscript, and I have a letter which proves this; that Harry had it bound and took it with him to New York last Fall, where he disposed of it. I have not got it in my possession and I do not know where it is now. If I had it I should be very glad to return it to you.

All Harry's affairs since his death are in the hands of his lawyers. If you want to get in communication with them, the man to write to is

> Raymond Harper
> 32, Avenue de L'Opera,
> Paris.

'THE ESCAPED COCK' was printed from a typewritten version and the manuscript which Harry had was something quite between Harry and Lawrence. All I know is that Harry would certainly not have had the manuscript bound and taken it to New York, if he had not believed that it belonged to him.

I regret very much that you could feel the way you wrote.
                    Very sincerely,
                    Caresse Crosby

3 Letters from Frieda Lawrence and Ada Lawrence Clarke to Martha Gordon Crotch*

[From Frieda]

Villa Bernarda
[Spotorno]
Prov di Genova

Tuesday [1930]

Dear Auntie—
Dear Old Serpent,

Here I am just with the child, a rough servant and I like it, to think, about things—It was jolly with you and I thank you so much—I am glad you seem full of beans—Keep the bean-supply up—I shall be able to write here and it was like this, when I was here with Lawrence—There is still so much to do in this life for me—

Still I'll float along, God knows what will carry me—

All my very best wishes
F——

Greet David very much from me and I thank him so much for everything—

See the tears? Please send this letter—

---

* In this chapter, to avoid confusion the name of the writer of each letter is given above the salutation.

[From Frieda]

Spotorno

Saturday
[? 1930]

My dear Auntie,

Of course I forgot my black coat with the green, do be an angel and send it me at once to Florence—It's all I have—I leave the 2 others with you—Capitano and I are alone here. I am just going to the market with the soldier—He is so human and nice with me and <u>real</u>, no high falute, but such a genuine warmth for me—I shall be allright—

Thank you, my dear

Hope Peter [Gordon] is trotting on his trotinette—

Love F
lots of it

[Peter Gordon was Mrs Crotch's nine-year old nephew. 'Capitano' was Angelo Ravagli.—eds]

[From Ada]

'Torestin'
Broadway
Ripley,
Derby

24 February 1931

My dear Auntie

When I saw your letter arrive today, I felt sure it was to say you had received the cardigan.

What a scandalous shame! I do feel sorry. I am going straight to the post-office now to enquire about it.

It is now three weeks last Saturday since it was posted off to you.

I wish now I had insured it.

If you don't get it I will send another and make sure of its safe arrival.

For three days now, we have had sunshine, and I feel I am just beginning to thaw.

I have been so busy—the garden, digging round the bulbs.

I've got such a lovely show of snowdrops, and hundreds of crocuses just waiting to burst open. I want to take some of the snowdrops to the grave at Eastwood. I can't believe a year is nearly gone since my brother died, and no real peace of mind have I had since.

If only things could be settled up favourably for Frieda, I should breathe freely again, but the thing drags on and on and I seem to be able to do so little.

Since my last big flare-up with my sister and brother nothing has been mentioned about the subject, and as I see George so little, I really don't know what he is doing at all.

Frieda writes desperate letters, imploring me to do this and that. She can explode like a mine, and sort of get it off her chest, but it worries me, and spoils my rest at night.

She knows I am absolutely for her, and would do anything in my power to help, but I can't interfere with lawyers, and agents, or compel my brother to do things.

It's so upsetting, I sometimes wish myself thousands of miles away. You see, it has not been very pleasant to go dead against my own flesh and blood, as I have, and I can assure you, I've got all the family against me, aunts and uncles included.

Not that they worry me at all—it's just that I can't <u>do</u> something that irritates.

I'm so thankful Frieda has got you—try to be with her at the week-end in case her thoughts are too much to bear.

> With love,
> Ada

[From Frieda]

Aboard S.S. Conte Grande

19 May 1931

My dear, dear——[Auntie]

So relieved I am. The man Philips sent a wire he would meet the boat—Bless him and you in case of difficulties— Tomorrow I land and then I'll spit on my hands and I wish I had you here—How often as 'me only 'ome'. I think of your Ritchee and you and also a charming young Lawrence enthusiast is coming to the ranch with me, <u>why</u> aren't you? I can't believe that I am as happy as I am after all the agony I have been through—I love you, my dear, for all your help and for what you are; and you'll be glad to know, that life is wonderful for me, quite newly so, after all, I'm a lucky bitch—and so are you! Because the Lord made us rich inside—

> Always my loving thoughts for you
> Frieda

I am sending that parcel tomorrow—gave Philips one of the Phoenix plates—He is a dear and loves you—

[From Frieda]   Prince George Hotel
                                                      [New York City]

                                                              Sunday
                                                              [1931]

Dear Auntie,

I thought I had posted this—I have done such a lot since I wrote this! Seen so many people and loved Mr Philips and a friend of his, Miss [Tessie] Payne—So friendly, everybody is and I think I shall be able to manage affairs—they want me to break the contract with Heinemann, that bullying Pollinger who thinks he knows best—I am with an Italian friend and I am coming to life again flying round in it and the pictures— Here is this nice drawing, don't you think it's nice? An english painter did it on board—When it was done, my first thought was to send it to the old serpent—I am enjoying the rest for my body—I wonder if there'll be anybody else in New York but I don't want anybody if Philips come to see me through—

> Love, I must pack—
> F

[From Ada]

'Torestin'
Broadway,
Ripley,
Derby.

21 May 1931

My dear Auntie
    I guessed you would understand how it was I had not written to you for so long.
    Since just before Easter, it has been one long rush with us—in fact, so much a rush, that we are all just about worn out.
    But one can't afford to lose any trade now-a-days with the competition so keen and the spender's money so limited. I could just do with a visit to you and one or two real heart to heart talks— but that is absolutely out of the question just now.
    We must see what can be arranged later on in the summer.
    I was delighted to know you had received both cardigans, and know you will make good use of them.
    Here, in England, it is impossible to do without them.
    Just fancy! nearly the end of May, and everybody shivering and shaking and going about with blue noses.
    I've got a glorious cold, and am almost sitting on top of the fire to write this.
    What a thrill you must have got out of the exhibition! I'm so thankful Frieda has left the pictures with you.
    It made me sad to see them piled round the walls of the villa.
    I wrote her a letter to Vence last week—not realizing she would be left. But I expect you can post it along for me.
    Things are still in a perfect muddle, and practically no progress is being made, and I for one, think that the best thing to do is to get the ruling of the court on the matter.
    But I want my attitude to be made quite clear, if it is taken to court.
    A letter of mine appeared in last week's 'Everyman' supporting the editor's review on 'Son of Woman'.
    I just said what I thought about Murry and have since had several letters from admirers of D. H. L., thanking me.
    Jack intends to write to you tonight—he is getting just about fed up but as the exam is in July he must stick to it. Fortunately he keeps fairly fit although he is so thin.

Please remember us to all the friends I met at your house and <u>do</u> write occasionally.

With love
Ada

×××
××× from Jack [Ada's elder son]

[From Ada]

[June 1931]

My dear [Auntie]

long time since I received your last letter—you will be thinking I have forgotten you.

If you only knew, how often Jack and I talk about you, and your kindness to us in Vence, you would realize, that you are one of the friends we shall never forget.

I picture you so often in your little shop and wish Jack and I could pop in for a word with you.

Is it very hot in Vence just how? We have had a fortnight of glorious weather, which has brought the flowers in our garden to perfection, and enabled us to have tennis to our hearts' content.

Today Jack starts his exam which lasts until next Tuesday week—Isn't it a long time?

The poor lad has been working night and day and is just about at the end . . .

[paragraph torn out, apparently by recipient]

. . .again.

I just received one letter, written as soon as she arrived in America and have had no word since.

I do hope she is alright. Pino sent two copies of the Apocalypse, one for myself and a signed copy for Jack.

It's a marvellous edition with such a charming photograph of Bert in front. But I expect you have already received one. Pino says he is now busy on my little book, so it may be out before so very long. You shall have a copy as soon as it is ready.

I wonder why Frieda never mentions any of her children to me now. Do you think Barby's illness had anything to do with it?

Jack wrote and thanked you for the antiques, didn't he?
They are helping to decorate his bedroom, which is now one mass of curios from floor to ceiling.

Do drop me a line when you can spare the time.

With combined love from Jack and myself.
Ada

[From Frieda] 14 [Lungarno] delle Grazie
Florence

Monday [1931]

Dearest Auntie,

What fun it will be to see you! I am so sorry to have left you that beastly mess! But I am <u>sure</u> he can do nothing and it's a try-on! Now I want you to think <u>whom</u> we could sell the pictures to or some of them—What about that American who varnished them? I want some money and I want you to have some—I asked the Aga Khan and he said he wanted to buy them, but <u>he</u> had no money to spare—What about the young Harmsworth—I think it was—I don't know yet where I shall spend Xmas—I am busy here with affairs, must then go to London and dread it, and the Capitano is miserable in his drill again! O dear, I wish we could <u>all</u> go to the ranch—it's the only possible life—How are you, my dear? They all send their love—I lunch with Pino, dine with the Aldingtons—They are bricks—

I feel I ought to come to you and see business through, but am so busy here and Richard helps—

I shall see you soon, My dear old serpent, <u>such</u> a mess my affairs are in—

Love
Frieda

[From Frieda]   14 Lungarno delle Grazie
Florence

[1931]

My dear Auntie,

I shall stay with the [Gair] Wilkinsons for Xmas, near the Mirenda—or I would have asked you to come—Anyhow I shall stay with you soon—I want to see you but nobody else in Vence, only the grave—So ask Thysson to help, really it's too monstrous of <u>Giraud</u>, he has done it before to some English <u>people</u>—Even [?]. How can the [?] possibly serve you with a [?] ? Do fight, Auntie dear, they will do it to the foreigners—He is well known to be a scoundrel. Ask Maestracci, I am <u>sure</u> he will advise you, and Thysson always helped. One must not give in to the swine—I cannot tell you, how sorry I am you have this bother, but you know that <u>agent</u> ought to help you. It was in his hands—Tell them you will fight and they are liars. Now, Auntie dear, I want you to send <u>me</u> of the typing of my book all you have and that play 'The fight for Barbara'. How are you off for money? I also am in a state of suspense and don't know where I am—About the pictures, perhaps it's a bad time for selling them except Americans—we'll talk about that when I come—

Have as good a Xmas as you can—
F

I would have come to you for Xmas but am so busy with Lawrence poems with Richard and my own book—Maestracci would help—Of course before you let the pictures go, pay the swine, but really why should one? Did you get my letter to you and Thysson and Giraud? And what about the agent? Serves the Riviera right for their <u>greed</u> if no foreigners come—, But you, my dear, are you all right? I long to see you at your place again—It's so cold and beastly here—

Ever yours,
Frieda

[From Frieda]   Kiowa Ranch
                                                       Taos
                                                New Mexico
                                               22 July 1931

My dear,
    Your letter was like a bumper glass of nectar—The latest my
dear, is that we have found <u>gold</u> on the ranch—It may be
nothing and it may be lots—I am awfully happy in spite of the
dirty, <u>mess</u> about L's work—You will know by now that the
Capitano Ravagli is with me, o scandal! We have been fond of
each other for years and that an old bird like me, is still capable
of real passion and can inspire it too, seems a miracle
especially after all the agony of Lawrence and my Barby—I
don't hear from her and I want too—But I hope things won't
turn into a tragedy; he, the capitano and I are getting too fond
of each other and as you know, there's the wife and the
children—But meanwhile it's marvelous to live here in
paradisal bliss, the horses, the marvelous free lovely place—
We work hard, we ride, I have a car and everybody says what a
woman full of vitality I am! (They won't say that in England,
alas!) I wish you were here! Of course, in New York instead of
going to the 'useful' swanks, I enjoyed myself with Philips and
his nice jolly friends! But I fought hard—Pollinger is so
rotten. Frere Reeves is a good one. We stuck if — But I am so
full of a new life, I just can't care about the lousy ones, Mabel
and Brett are lovely with me now that Lorenzo is dead — How
is the grave? I can't bear to think of him, there, under the
ground and I am going it, full tilt, but he would have wanted
me to, I know — When you have been married to a Lawrence,
you can't be put on the shelf, till you are put there for
good — O dear, are there any female [?] left in Vence? How
depressing for you—Had a nice letter from Sedgwick. Lord,
but it's wonderful here! Have I left you enough money for the
insurance?
    Tell me, if you hear from Barby—
    A thousand good wishes and all my gratitude to you always,
    Be nice to the Ravagli woman!

                                    Frieda

[From Ada]   'Torestin',
                                                Broadway,
                                                Ripley,
                                                Derby.

14 December 1931

My dear Auntie,

I had delayed answering your first letter, until I could send our Xmas Greetings, and now I find you still worried over this wretched business.

Jack has translated his paper to me, and although as you say, these men are swindlers, yet, I really don't think 3000 Frs. an exorbitant price to ask for compensation for damage done. When I wrote Frieda urging her to put things to right straight away, she answered, saying she would write you immediately.

Why didn't she send a cheque to you at once, so that you could settle things?

If it is possible to settle for less than the amount they claim, I should be inclined to do so, even if the 3000 Frs. has to be paid. But you want to make sure that no further claims will be made and that everything is satisfactorily cleared up.

If you do so, let me know at once what you have had to find and I will get Frieda to send you on a cheque for that amount.—She must not evade her responsibilities in this way.

I will take good care that you suffer no loss.

Now about my book—Last Monday I received a letter from Orioli saying that 'Young Lorenzo' was in the hands of the binders and would be ready in a few days.—Then like a bolt from the blue a cable sent by Pollinger to him, stating that as Heinemann had bought the copyright of all letters and unpublished material, they threatened an injunction against Orioli if he published.

Now I believe Pollinger is at the bottom of all this, because, when I wrote and explained that we had obtained written permission to publish from George and Frieda, he replied that he could make things alright with both Heinemann and Secker and would try to place the book in England and America for a cheaper publication later.

That means of course, that if we have him as agent, so that he can get his 10% commission everything will be alright but otherwise we are bunkered.

It's a damnable position to be in—at the mercy of a swine like he is, but as he seems to have absolute control over the Lawrence estate and everybody else, we shall have to bow to the inevitable and let him handle the book for us.

I'm very anxious to see it, and hope it will be liked. I'm enclosing a cutting out of last Thursday's 'Times Literary Supplement'.

Last week Jack had his first article published in the school magazine.

I thought it very good, but he is over modest about it, and will show it to nobody.

We are busy preparing for Xmas puddings—cakes etc, but somehow I don't feel in a very festive mood. The depressing state of the country effects one's spirits, and although we mustn't grumble where our little business is concerned, yet things could be so much easier.

My sister and family are taking up poultry farming—an entirely new venture for them, and I hope their little capital will not be lost.

I had not seen George for about eight months until last Monday—when I had to find out about Heinemann and the copyright. He sounded fed up with the whole business. I see now that he is perfectly helpless in some of the matters Frieda accuses him of doing.

Like she, he is tied hopelessly and helplessly by signing that contract; and the agent Pollinger and the publishers seem to do just what they like.

The lawyers too are dragging things on indefinitely and nothing will be settled until Frieda comes back and takes the thing to law.

I see in the papers where Sir Hugo de Beers is married and to a grandmother too.

Do they ever come back to Vence?

Jack and I are sending you a small parcel tomorrow together with our love.

We wish we were coming to Vence, as we did last year, but must wait until conditions are better.

Take care of yourself.

With affectionate greetings from us all.
Ada

[From Ada]   'Torestin',
                                              Broadway,
                                              Ripley,
                                              Derby.

                                        18 January 1932

My dear Auntie

I'm sorry to have kept you so long waiting for a reply, but have been so worried over Jack.

For a week or two preceding Xmas, he was not well, and finally had to take to his bed a fortnight ago.

I thought he was in for pneumonia, but the doctor said it was bronchial catarrh. He had a frightful cough and we had to poultice back and front for two days.

He's much better now, and just able to get out-of-doors, but seems so weak and looks ghastly.

On Thursday I am taking him up to London to a chest specialist to be thoroughly examined.

I'm so afraid when I look at him, for he reminds me so much of Bert at his age.

It's very disappointing for the boy too, because he's fretting to get back to school, but I'm determined he shall be quite fit before he starts studying again.

I have written to Bournemouth to some people I know, and they are quite willing to board him for a week or two; but first of all he must see the specialist.

Has Orioli sent you a copy of 'Young Lorenzo'?

I have written asking him to do so and hope you will like it.

Just fancy Frieda being in London too!

I was amazed when I got her letter, for she told me she was going from Florence to Vence.

Has she settled that affair yet?

I have wondered many times.

She wrote asking me to go to London at once, but I can't leave my home and responsibilities like that.

I shall see her when I take Jack, but shall not be able to stay, as he needs looking after carefully.

But I'm hoping the wretched estate business can be settled up and am ready to fight on her side when necessary.

[Letter incomplete.]

[From Ada]   'Torestin',
                                                        Broadway,
                                                        Ripley,
                                                        Derby.

                                                  26 February 1932

Dear Auntie

I'm so sorry we have kept you waiting so long for news, but as I didn't take Jack to London until last week end, I couldn't write much earlier.

Well! Things turned out much better than I anticipated. The doctor sounded him thoroughly and said there was nothing seriously wrong with him, but that he was very weak chested, with a tendency for lung trouble.

He thinks that with care and treatment the lad should grow strong, but advises the open air as much as possible for him.

After seeing the doctor, we went straight to the Kingsley Hotel and stayed with Frieda until the train time. She looks remarkably well and younger than ever; and is having a very wonderful time, seeing all sorts of people and being generally made a great deal of.

The estate business did not come off as we thought, a fortnight ago, and now the lawyers think it might drag on until July.

Frieda's lawyer, Medley, of Field Roscoe & Co., is representing me also, and Robinson stands for George and Emily. It's a complicated business and the sooner it is all settled the better.

Secker is publishing an expurgated edition of Lady Chatterley's Lover and the orders are pouring in in thousands.

I wonder if my brother would have liked it—I very much doubt it.

I mentioned the Vence trouble to Frieda and urged her to offer the hussie part of the money and get it settled.

She has got plenty of money, and should get the matter straightened out.

This is a very hurried letter, written at the shop.

                      Love from Jack and Ada

[From Ada]   'Torestin',
                                               Broadway,
                                               Ripley,
                                               Derby.

                                            11 June 1932

My dear Auntie

You will be wondering at my long silence, but, I hope, not thinking I have forgotten you.

We have just got over our rush in the business, and now I can pull up a little of my correspondence.

Considering the bad state of trade in the country, we have done remarkably well, but really, business now-a-days is a frightful worry and I'm always selfish enough to wish I could manage without it.

I'm sorry things have been so slack with you—let us hope the next season will be much better.

You quite take my breath away with the wonderful idea of the theatre etc. I actually saw a reference to it in one of the daily papers, with the name of the wealthy man who offered to finance it.

Have you done anything further about it? I am frightfully interested and think it would be a perfect memorial to my brother.

Frieda is in London as you know but I have not yet seen her.

She promised to come straight away to Ripley, but kept putting it off, so I've told her not to worry.

To tell you the truth, I've put up with so many insulting references to the family that I'm tired of it, and when she writes to say we don't appreciate her sufficiently—that Bert got his genius from her, she made him what he was and all sorts of piffle, I just write and tell her what I think of her.

The homage paid to her, as the widow of D.H.L.—goes to her head, and fills her with a false sense of self importance.

I don't mind that, and am really glad she is getting such a thrill out of life, but she must leave the family alone, and not try to destroy my memories of my brother.

It's made me very sad, for I had hoped she could fill Bert's place in my life, but it's impossible. Don't think I'm telling tales, but I want you to know my side in case Frieda says anything; and I know you'll understand.

Jack keeps much better in health—is now 5 ft. 8 in., and begins to make me look small.

He takes a big exam again in July, but I doubt whether he will get through; for you see he has been away from school nearly a whole term.

I have had many interesting letters from readers of 'Young Lorenzo'. Last week, one came from a student [Harry T. Moore] in Chicago.

He is making a Grand Tour and hopes to visit Vence and the grave.

I gave him your address, so don't be surprised at a visit some time in July.

He is coming to Ripley and I am going to show him the Lawrence country.

This week, my husband and I are going to Ascot for two days, and I'm keenly looking forward to it.

It is the one race-meeting I like best during the year, and I always get a thrill out of the lovely creations there.

I wish you could see my garden just now.

It's a wonderful sight, with the laburnum, lilac, and other flowering shrubs in full bloom. Give me my garden and family, and I'm quite content.

My sister and her husband are running a poultry farm four miles from Newark.

It's a beautiful place, and I hope they will be able to make it pay.

I've not seen my brother George for 8 or 9 months, but hear he has not been very well.

No news yet of the case. I shall be glad when it is over. Have you read 'Lorenzo—Taos' by Mabel Luhan? It is not very flattering to Frieda.

> Love from Jack and myself
> Ada

[From Ada]   'Torestin',
                                              Broadway,
                                              Ripley,
                                              Derby.

                                         16 July 1932

My dear Auntie

Thanks so much for your kind and sympathetic letter.

I know you fully understand how matters are but are too loyal a friend to take sides with either party.

Besides, why should you. I have had no further communication with Frieda and think it better, this silence, than the hurtful letters that were always passing to and fro.

What a painful time you have been experiencing too! People in trouble invariably find you out and demand more of you than is reasonable.

You must learn to harden your heart a little, or you will be worn out.

Now I am going to tax your good nature further—just to the extent of giving a cup of tea to a young American friend of mine, who will be in Nice for a day or two and is anxious to see the grave.

He wrote to me from Chicago after reading my book, and expressed a desire to see the Lawrence country.

I invited him to stay with us for a day or two, and my husband motored us about in Nottinghamshire and Derbyshire, and young Mr [Harry T.] Moore was absolutely delighted.

You will like him immensely for he has a most remarkable brain and understands D.H.L.'s philosophy perfectly.

While in London he met Frieda, Kotorliansky, Cath Carswell and Murry, but thinks Koteliansky has the brains of them all.

He knows your friend Emma Goldman, so I hope you will have much in common.

I had a nice letter from Brigit Patmore the other day— Some day I should like to meet her.

Jack is keeping fairly well, but ready for the holidays which commence next week. He may be going to Germany for a week year to study at the university at Bonn, where my Uncle Fritz [Krenkow] is a professor.

We shall decide when Uncle comes over next month.

In a fortnight's time we go on a caravan tour of the North and South Coast of Devon.

I am keenly looking forward to it, and the children do nothing else but make plans. I guess it is very hot on the riviera just now. We have had wonderful weather and everybody is already asking if I have been on my holidays.

I wish I could send you flowers and fruit out of my garden. It is such a joy to gather one's own strawberries etc.

I have not heard how the Lawrence case is getting on.

Field Roscoe have not written for months, but as I agree fully to whatever Frieda wishes in the matter, I suppose there is no need.

At any rate, I'm not troubling much what happens.

Trade is quiet with us just now. Sales are in full swing, but the miners are working so badly that even bargains are beyond their pockets.

It's nice you have had a pleasant companion in the little boy.

Jack would have liked to meet him.

Tell me what you think about Mr Moore.

Yours Sincerely
Ada

Jack <u>sends love</u>

[From Ada]   'Torestin',
                                                         Broadway,
                                                         Ripley,
                                                         Derby.

7 September 1932

My dear Auntie

It's always such a joy to hear from you, for your letters are so bright and full of interesting little items.

I'm afraid mine in comparison seem very dull and full of woe.

Now first of all, will you please get me flowers with the money enclosed.

Bert's birthday falls on the 11th of this month, and I would like his grave to look nice for that day.

I know you won't mind doing this for me.

You ask me how things are concerning Frieda and the case. Well! I'll try to explain just what has been happening.

I believe I told you about our 'difference' of some months ago.

For several weeks I refused to have anything to do with her, but when she finally offered me the olive branch and apologised to some extent, I again corresponded with her.

Then she dropped a bomb-shell on me by saying that Emily and George were demanding £700 each together with some Mss. before they could renounce their claims to the estate.

I was in a terrible way, and rushed off to Nottingham to see them both.

It was a deliberate lie. The offer had come from Frieda's solicitor and was £500 for each of them.

They even went to the extent of sending Pollinger over to Nottingham with a cheque already made out and the dirty dog tried to threaten him into accepting, and said I was to get pictures and Mss.

You can guess how furious I was at this dirty and dishonest method of bribery on Frieda's part.

I told both Emily and George they would lose not only their own self-respect; but the respect of all decent people if they accepted Frieda's terms.

Then I said to them 'Now what do you really want, or feel entitled to'; and their reply was 'nothing during Frieda's life and only the copy-rights at her death'.

Well, I thought that was surely reasonable enough, they were taking nothing from her and most people seem to be of the opinion that the copy-rights should go back to his family at her death.

I thought she would be delighted to have things settled so reasonably, but apparently I was wrong, for she now accuses me of greed, and wanting everything for myself.—says I've been playing a double game for my own ends and a lot more filth that I will spare you hearing.

What I cannot understand is this—She says Bert never wanted George to have any of his belongings and yet she is prepared to part with £1000 of my brother's money in order to be rid of the family.

Now which is the most decent solution—mine, by which she

loses nothing during her life-time, or hers by which £1,000 of Bert's money is used for bribery.

No, I'm glad I put a scotch in her wheel.

She's blackened our family enough as it is, but what would she have said to the world if they had taken her money.

If I were starving tomorrow, I would refuse to touch sixpence belonging to her; and I've finished trying to be decent any more.

For his sake I've put up with more insults, than I ever thought possible, but it's ended now. I shall not write any more, or answer any of her letters.

My position regarding the case is still the same, I shall support the claim as I always intended, for I know what Bert would have me do, but as I say to Emily and George 'if you feel you are entitled to the copy rights, well let the law decide for you'.

Don't think I want you to take sides with her. I'm just giving you the facts of the case, and it's well for you to know both sides, for I've no doubt you will get Frieda's story sooner or later.

I've ordered that book by Emma Goldman and am looking forward to reading it.

I'm glad you liked young Moore, and were able to introduce him to such interesting people [Emma Goldman, Alexander Berkman, Mrs Frank Harris].

What an experience meeting Elvira Barney! What a vicious type some of these young moneyed people are—no good to themselves or anyone else. They certainly should be made to work for their living. Some friends have just popped in so I must close

With much love
Ada

[From Frieda]

10 Hammersmith Terrace
Hammersmith

[1932]

Dear Auntie,

Well, I was glad to get your news—I have too many [sic], so I'll leave it till I see you and that may be quite soon—So be prepared and be cheerful—Tell David I hope he'll meet me when I come and give him my love—

How queer about Elvira Barney and about Lawrence—It's his birthday on the 11th, don't forget—What a mess the world is in! I am not well and I am not happy here—I hope there's nothing wrong with my inside—This is a mournful letter, but underneath I'm allright—Barby comes, is well, but always a trial to herself—She has an idea I ought to go back to Ernest! God help him then—

Hope you are well—I'm not and cross about it—

Ever yours
F

[From Frieda]   Kingsley Hotel
                                                               Hart Street
                                                            London WC1

                                                                  [1932]

Dearest Auntie,

There, I had to come in a hurry—I was sorry not to come and see you and the grave—Of course you'll be quite equal to dealing with the pictures, don't let them go, that's all—I know the others would help you and I could pay afterwards naturally—I wonder if you have sold those two—I came to fight, claiming there was a will and I think I shall win—Medley, the lawyer very good and keen—but by the time I've paid all the lawyers there won't be much left—Alas, but still to be free would be a treat—Saw Barby, she is well and happy—she has done some good work—See lots of people, everybody charming with me—Aldous and Maria, Ottoline, Frere, but it's depressing I can tell you, a beastly fog to-day—dark as hell—Hope you are not too depressed—I am so busy, seeing people and this fight—but it does one good—

So help me, Auntie dear, and hang on to the pictures—I am sure you get some fun out of that nephew—

Ever yours
F

[From Frieda]   Kingsley Hotel
                                                  Hart Street
                                                  WC1

                                                  Tuesday
                                                  [? 7 Nov 1932]
Dear Auntie,

Really, Auntie, I cannot tell you <u>how</u> deeply triumphant I feel (I touch wood!). I wasn't sure of winning not till the case came on; a severe old judge, Lord Merivale; but I pulled all my force together in the witness box, just went ahead, felt I could convince crocodiles that Lawrence wanted me to have his inheritance—They say I <u>was</u> convincing—But the triumph was <u>Lorenzo's</u>: The judge said: 'This very distinguished man' and treated *me* with such respect—you see this old Merivale wanted to sort of pay respect to Lawrence after all the persecution—I still feel a bit <u>drunk</u>—And the way Lawrence is pervading this England now is just surprising, I am full of the deepest satisfaction for <u>his</u> sake—I have not lived in vain—So there's a song of triumph for you—

And Barby is quite well—Fatter and sane and rosy—Elsa is having a child and happy and Monty too is happy—So really there's no more to desire for me on God's earth—<u>nothing</u>—

But now to you—I thought of you at the trial and it cost me so much strength and self control and Murry helped me and Medley and I could *not* stand it another time. Had it lasted longer I would have collapsed. Can you stand the ordeal? <u>I</u> had only George as opponent and was terribly lucky—But you have the medical profession, who will fight against you tooth and nail! You have so little <u>chance</u> and is it worth your strength? You might collapse, I think I would in your case—that man will <u>never</u> admit he left scissors inside you— But could you not try to get some money out of him? My Medley was wonderful too, made it all so <u>clear</u> to me—But Ada is <u>furious</u> naturally—

I feel almost <u>uncanny</u>, so <u>free</u>! I can understand how you hate this terrible injustice and injury that has been done to you—But, oh, the fight is <u>terrible</u>, Auntie and people are wild beasts and inhuman—And you <u>must</u> not lose—Lawrence protected me you see—Who would really care about you?

Tell Maestracci [doctor at Vence] my good news—Barby is really well—I am sorry he has had an operation, but glad he has a rest—Went to the G. B. Shaws', liked <u>her</u> so much—I wonder if you'll come—I liked Stella Churchill—Am so busy and seeing lots of people—Couldn't you leave Peter at Vence? You'd be more free alone—

Ever yours
F

[From Ada]

'Torestin',
Broadway,
Ripley,
Derby.

12 November 1932

My dear Auntie

I really feel ashamed I have kept you waiting so long for a letter, but when you know what a worrying time I have had, I know you will forgive me.

I felt somehow, I couldn't write until this family business had been settled, and I could tell you definitely one thing or another.

Perhaps you have seen the 'case' in 'The Times', where I am wrongly put down as a defendant along with Emily and George, and made a participator in the 'generous settlement'.

You know perfectly well I have never made any claim on my brother's estate, and in common justice to me my position should have been made quite clear in the press.

It's been a sordid business all through, and I blame Frieda very much for not making the only decent settlement, of leaving the copyright to Emily and George at her death.

Huxley, Orioli, and all his real friends, said that was the best way out, and I'm sure the way Bert would have wished, but just because I suggest it, I'm told I'm doing it for my own benefit.

She forced Emily and George into accepting the money and Mss. because they have no courage, and were threatened with having to pay all costs, but I tell you candidly, that if I had felt as they do, I should have fought the case.

As it is, they have sold their self-respect and tarred the whole family for filthy money.

I feel I've finished with the lot of them—they none of them

have realised the honesty and integrity of Bert and have stooped to meannesses undreamed of.

I've written and told Frieda just what I think of the whole rotten business and never to write to me again. The day after the case came off, she wrote saying what a triumph it had been for my brother and offering me his picture of the Holy Family, hoping it was worth £500.

I told her the triumph was Frieda Lawrence's not Bert's, and that she had better keep the picture, as she might need £500 more than I.

Apparently my letter went home, for Middleton Murry is now trying to reunite us as he calls it, and offering to come and see me.

It is not a bit of use, for Frieda's outlook on life is so different, and we both have a different interpretation for such words as decency etc.

She's got her own way—let her be satisfied, and leave me alone.

I'm enclosing two holiday snaps. One—the caravan in which we spent a heavenly fortnight touring Devonshire. On it you will see my husband and Jack and Bertie, and a friend of ours.

The other one is very good of Jack, and not so bad of Bertie either.

How I wish I could unburden myself to you for a time. I feel sure it would do me good to have a long talk with you, and then perhaps I could get rid of this sore throat. I've gone through hell since he died and I begin to lose faith in the decency of those I cared most for. Some day though, I shall run over to see you—if only for a fortnight.

Yesterday I had such a nice letter from the young American [Harry T. Moore] so appreciative for what I did, and offering us such a warm welcome to America.

He says how kind you were to him and how thrilled he was to see Vence and meet your friends.

Secker is bringing out the cheap edition of my book this week—it looks quite nice, but the reproductions are not so good.

A girl named Louie Burrows to whom Bert was unofficially engaged for a short time, has objected to the casual way she is mentioned in the book and has threatened to take action.

She is the 'Ursula' of 'The Rainbow', and after waiting all

these years for revenge suddenly decides to have it upon me.

As the reference to her is so slight, and not in the least libellous, we have told her to get on with the job.

But all these little unpleasantnesses upset one, and coming on the top of the other trouble make one rather fed up.

Trade is still very bad everywhere, and we have just had another coal-mine close down in our district, which has thrown another 500 men out of employment.

We have to be thankful just to keep going.

Next year, Jack goes to a university—I don't know which, for Cambridge is out of the question now he refuses to take Latin.

He should have gone to Bonn with my uncle, who is a professor there, but decided instead to stay on at school and take the High School Certificate.

We must wait and see what the future has in store for him.

How did you get on with the case you talked of opening again?

It is a wicked shame they should get off scot-free, after mutilating you in that fashion.

Now I must 'dry up' and attend to business.

Hoping yours are well and happy.

With love,
Ada

[From Ada]

'Torestin',
Broadway,
Ripley,
Derby.

20 December 1932

My dear Auntie

What a surprise to get your letter and to know you are in England.

You will enjoy an English Xmas again, and be happy in the midst of your own folk.

If you can't manage to get so far as Ripley, perhaps we could arrange to meet for a short time in London after Xmas.

I could get a half-day excursion, which gets in to London somewhere about 2.30 p.m. and need not leave until midnight.

Perhaps you will see what you can do.

Of course I should love you to come here for a few days, but will leave it with you.

We are expecting quite a number of folk this Xmas and Boxing day, and I'm really looking forward to a little gaiety, after the miserable time I have had.

I've put Frieda quite out of my mind—for I cannot follow her in any way. Her methods, and way of living are totally opposed to mine, and she will be perfectly happy without my friendship.

I may sound a bit puritanical to you, but there are limits to one's tolerance, and I know more than you can guess.

She has her children, although I doubt whether they mean much, so let her be just what she likes—it is better so.

Trade is rotten, but every body is in the same boat, so we mustn't complain too much.

What a blessing the little boy's father has got something to do—this unemployment is terrible.

Here's wishing you everything of the best; and may you really prosper in the New Year as you deserve.

> With love
> Ada

[From Frieda]   Buenos Aires

8 February [1934]

Dear Auntie,

4 years nearly that Lorenzo is dead—Think of his grave on the first.

Here I am seeing the world, and I like it—I hear Barby may come to you—She seems well—

Just a word, to enclose this cheque—How are you?

Shall be back at the ranch in April—then my book comes out—I'll send it to you—

I wish things were easier for all my friends and relations—that is my only thought, and the world in a mess—All the more reason <u>somebody</u> should be well—and go on as happily as possible—

O dear, I hate to think of Lawrence in his little grave—but how the wings of his spirit have spread—He is read here a great deal, but no money for me—

All very best wishes, dear Auntie

Yours
Frieda

[From Ada]   'Torestin,'
Broadway,
Ripley,
Derby.

Sunday
14 May 1935

My dear Auntie

You've no idea how glad and yet how guilty I felt when your letter arrived.

I ought to have written to you long before this, but somehow I couldn't settle down to write to anybody.

After the hateful business with Frieda last year, I felt I would like to be in some unknown spot and have no contact with the outside world at all.

And now I'm months behind with my correspondence and yet have very little time to pull up.

After a very depressing winter season, we have been quite busy—so rushed, in fact, that since Easter, we have been obliged to work each Sunday until 1.30 a.m.

I am really amazed, for only this last month, over a thousand miners have received their notices, and the same thing has happened all round the district.

But how nice it is to be busy once more, even if one gets dog tired and irritable. I guess I wasn't cut out for a lady's life.

It makes me miserable to think things are so bad your way, and you have tried so hard too.

The gods have not been very kind to you, have they? and yet you manage to extract more out of life than so many of the stodgy people I come in contact with.

I was glad Jack wrote to you from Germany.

He went to Bonn for a fortnight, to interview certain professors with a view to entering the university next October.

An uncle of mine, who is professor of Islamic languages there, is retiring at the end of July, and was very keen Jack should look round the place while he was there.

Jack is very anxious to get into a publisher's office, and Bert's friend Koteliansky thought it would be a good idea to enter the university at Bonn, which is considered the best in Germany.

Middleton Murry called unexpectedly on Good Friday, with the intention I believe, of trying to make peace between Frieda and myself.

But he changed his mind after Eddie (my husband) in very lurid language, said what he thought of Frieda and her behaviour to me.

I said very little for I very much doubt the honesty of purpose of so many of the so-called friends of Bert and Frieda, but I made it quite clear that so far as I am concerned I shall never again let Frieda play even the smallest part in my life.

She is very happy in her role as the wonderful woman who made Bert what he was, she also has plenty of money, and will never want, and on the whole is getting a much bigger kick out of life than ever she got while he lived.

In my little way, I, too, am quite happy—can always earn my own living, and don't expect I shall be dependent on anyone—so why should I trouble about Frieda or her doings.

Believe me, unless her name is mentioned in letters or by visitors like Murry, we never even think about her, and it's much the best way.

She told Murry, I was just as keen after the money as the others, and he also said how she hated me, but strange to say, it didn't move me in the slightest.

I don't care sufficiently to worry about any doings of hers.

My brother George has been very ill—heart-trouble of some kind.

I went to see him once, but felt so strange just as if he were the biggest stranger.

Although he is only eight miles away, I have only seen him that once this year.

Now with my sister, it is very different. Her husband has a lovely poultry farm in a quaint little village not far from Newark and I love to go and help with the chickens and pigs etc.

When we retire, I think I shall set up a few fowls and live the simple life.

I'm going to enclose a snap, so that you can see how Jack has grown.

I wish you could see our garden just now—it is looking perfectly lovely with all the Spring flowers.

How nice to have your niece with you—I guess she will cause a few hearts to flutter.

How does the grave look, and does Frieda pay the caretaker to have it looked after? Will you please let me know, for if not, I will arrange to have it kept tidy like the family grave at Eastwood.

Write to me again when you have time. With affectionate greetings from everybody.

Ada

[From Frieda]   [San Cristóbal, New Mexico]

[1935]

Dear Auntie,

I thought you would be angry! It is the limit—But I didn't care after an hour or two! Because it's too canaille!

I wrote to [Sir Thomas] Dunlop (an old friend and Inspector General of British consulates)—and [Earl] Brewster to send me Lawrence here; we have made a lovely place on the hill, a bit like the little temple of Isis in 'The Escaped Cock'.

—Am enjoying doing it—Have been very happy this summer, especially as all is well with Barby and Elsa—Monty—

I often think of Vence and you—Who do you think is here: Burke—I liked Mrs Perry—

She wrote simply awfully nice things about my book—Hope you get it—safely—

It looks like snow to-day—We shall kill the pigs soon—I like to think you are living in the place over the shop, it was so friendly—

But I am happy here with this natural life, baking my bread and doing things all the time—Bother too, I have, but who hasn't? I run into the woods and forget it—

The Vence news are welcome but I wish the French were nicer about money, they are nice in so many ways—

But that [?] is the limit—I could prosecute them and make them pay—

[Remainder of letter missing.]

[From Frieda]   St. Joseph's Hospital
                                                 Albuquerque

                                              19 March 1935

Dear Auntie,
    Of course I am not cross with you, you always did what you could—And have been very good to me—I have just nearly died of double pneumonia, but am much better again—Have not got my strength yet back—
    Angelino had Lawrence cremated and wants to bring the ashes back to the ranch, where we have built a lovely little chapel—But you'll still look after the grave won't you? L's first resting place—I <u>am</u> glad he is no longer there—Glad to hear all your news, this is a short but friendly note—I am still feeble

                          Yours with love
                                Frieda

[From Frieda]   Kiowa Ranch

                                                2 May 1935

Dear Auntie,
    Angelino gratefully says you made it possible for him to come here!
    I am glad you liked him! He is working now in the little chapel!
    My great news is that Barby with husband is coming early in June! How lovely it will be to see her and she will adore it here! All good wishes to you!

                            Ever yours,
                                Frieda

4 Letters from Angelo Ravagli to Martha Gordon Crotch

Via IV Novembre 3/6
Savona

16 March 1935

Dear Madame,

The ashes of Lawrence is all ready. I can take it any time—But yesterday I am going to American consulate in Geneva and I having not found the vice consulate, the consulate generale don't want give me a answer, and I want to spet till Thursday when can bak from vacation the vice consulate.

In the mean time I have send telegram to Frieda because she interesting the American consulate at give me the visa for made the special and delicate mission—

Barbara tell me know that she can do anything because the American Consulate from London he won't have to have confirmation from Geneva—

My trip it was good—my family too—Thanks very much for your good help, my rispetly to Mr Garnet[t] and to you many wishes from me at my wife—

Sincerely yours
Angelo Ravagli

Via IV Novembre 3/6
Savona

25 March 1935

Dear Mrs Crotch–

I am ready now. I go take the boath at Villefranche at 4 April with the Lawrence's ashes—with the 'Cente di Savoia'. Many thanks for your good help and for the photographs to you and to Mr Garnet[t]—

I arived to New York at 11 April and in the Ranch—about at 15—I have telegraph to Frieda and I think she is happy.

Mr Aldous Huxley has not write to me, but I have obtaine same the famous visa and I am all ready now—

My family is good, my wife return to you the best regards—

Many salutations, Madame, and my good wishes to you and to Mr Garnet[t].

I am sincerely yours
Angelo Ravagli

5 Letters between Frieda Lawrence and Richard Aldington

[1932]

Dear Richard,

I never told you <u>enough</u> how I am so very pleased about that introduction of Lorenzo's [*Etruscan Places*]— It's also so alive and good and unliterary—And I am terribly grateful to you, for saying it all—and in that form—I do wish you would conquer that throat, but perhaps it's something evil, that your soul wants to get rid of—It is so rotten that it won't get well—Make it get better! I'll burn a candle with Pino for you—

We do want you to be well—
F

Vence

Saturday [1932]

Dear Richard,
Dear Brigit [Patmore],

I sent your letter to George—I thought it might make him see things—

I almost wept tears of joy over that heavenly jacket—It was so adorable of you all to send it me—Yes, indeed, what a good time we had—you must come here, the climate is so good and if we don't have quite so much fun, you can be peaceful and work—

I am very grateful Pino is going to help, I hope he is not sacrificing too much—Ada is nice, you must know her one day—Richard, you are very encouraging about the book [Lawrence's *Letters*, ed. A. Huxley]—I hope we shall all

73

flourish like the bay-tree—I am reading Lawrence's letters a boil how poor we were and how it worried him, living from hand-to-mouth, a few pounds at a time—Poor, poor Lorenzo—his poor pride, how it suffered—Eddie Marsh trying to tell him, how he should write his poetry! [metrical] Feet you know— — —I want to give him 'feet', only he wouldn't have real ones, anyhow!

Glad you are all feeling gay! Auntie feels, she has been in another world, among the 'élite'. So she has, my word!

Tanti, tanti saluti, to you, Richard and that lamb of a Brigit—

I daren't put on my jacket, except when I have had a very hot, scented bath—

Love
Frieda

Apt 518
The Dupont Circle
Connecticut Avenue at Dupont Circle
Washington, D. C.

19 December 1940

Dear Frieda,

I was very pleased indeed to have your letter, and glad to know that you were interested in the memoirs. The Atlantic only printed extracts from the book, which is going to be called Life for Life's Sake. I have told my publishers to send you a copy as soon as the book is ready.

Do you remember our Christmas with Pino in Florence, ten years ago now? Poor Pino! I wonder what has happened to him. I have written to everyone I can think of, but get no news. Norman, I hear from Willy Maugham, is in unoccupied France, and will probably not have a very nice life. Auntie is in New York.

You were very sensible to leave Europe. It is all murderously rotten, as Lorenzo said it was. I got out two years ago—nine months before the war started—and already it was dreadful.

Indeed, it would be wonderful to see you again, and talk over old times. I should like to start right away! But I am working at the huge Congressional Library here on a big 'literary' book for a publisher which I have to do, because I can get no money from England or the Continent. But I hope to get it finished within the next two months.

Moreover, since I saw you, I have been divorced by H.D., married again, and have a beautiful little girl of two and a half. Netta, my wife, has read Lorenzo's books over and over, and is longing to see you. But there is the question of the little girl. The main point is whether climate and conditions in New Mexico are such that it would be safe to bring her there, say, in February or March. Would it be possible for us to find a small place not too far from you, with running water, means of heating, and an ice-box for milk? (I could get an ice-box, I suppose.) And is it possible to get fresh milk?

I have a car, rather an old one, but I think it would make the journey. If you are sure the conditions would be all right for Catherine, we would love to make the trip as soon as this old book is finished. Perhaps if I got away from the mechanical East for a few months I could write something creative again. Anyway, it sounds like a real adventure to go to New Mexico by car, and above all to see you.

Will you let me know what you think, especially about the practical side. I could afford to pay up to 75 dollars a month rent, but may be that is too little in N.M.? I know nothing about prices there.

Frere is in the government service, and a close aid of Bevin, the Labour Minister. Charles Prentice is back at Chattos. I hear nothing of Brigit. I believe Hilda is in London; at any rate she was soon after the war started.

How boring all this war is! It is awful and murderous and destructive, but the boredom of it is what strikes me. It would be too humiliating to try to live under such conditions.

With love,
Richard

P.S. We could talk about the Lady C. script, if it proved possible for us to come out. What worries me about it is the almost complete impossibility of making a film without utterly changing the whole meaning of the book. They would make it sentimental, I fear.

R

Dupont Circle Hotel
Connecticut Avenue
Washington, D. C.

16 January 1941

Dear Frieda,

I should have written sooner, but we've all been having colds.

We feel more and more that we would like to spend some time in New Mexico this year, if it can be arranged. There are several things Netta wants me to ask you before we absolutely and finally decide. They don't matter to us so much as our little girl.

(1) Is it possible to get a doctor in any emergency; and how long does it take?

(2) Are there snakes and scorpions; and, if so, can you tell us how to treat Catherine if she should be bitten?

(3) Can we get fresh fruit and vegetables fairly regularly?

(4) How is the cooking done? On charcoal or wood fire? And what is the lighting?

This sounds awfully fussy, but we want to be prepared for everything. If there are things we should bring, will you tell us?

Personally I am simply longing to get away. The war has descended on this town like a great pall—it feels as England did when we left two years ago.

How soon do you think it would be wise for us to come? Of course, I shall be quite ready to pay the 50 dollars monthly for the house, and to buy milk, eggs, chickens and bread and any other farm stuff from you. As it is such a long way, would you consider letting us have an option on the house from April to October? We couldn't afford to come just for a few weeks; but in six months I might be able to do some writing. Here it is only possible to do mechanical stuff, but I have practically finished the big book, and it would be so heavenly to get away from cities and back to our kind of life again.

We have been thinking these last few days that the easiest way to take our baggage and at the same time have a sleeping place always ready for Catherine, is to buy a trailer. Would it be possible to get it up to the ranch? That would solve a lot of problems for us.

Do let me hear soon. It will be so wonderful to think that in a few weeks we shall actually be starting off.

Ever yours,
Richard

P.S.   I have put several of Lorenzo's poems into my anthology, and of course you will be paid a fee for each one.

Dupont Circle Apts
Connecticut Avenue
Washington, D.C.

1 February 1941

Dear Frieda,
    I enclose with this a letter for Angelino. It was so nice of him to write and to give all that information.
    I don't know when we can get away from here. I have to write something else for the book I have done for Viking Press. And then I have to arrange to be 'put' somewhere to correct the proofs, probably in April or May. It is an enormous job, an anthology of English and American poetry, over 1500 pages. I hope there is a small room I can work in, as I shall have to start another book as soon as possible. We have to be very economical, as I don't write for the movies or the popular magazines; and of course there is not a penny to be had from England or the Continent. And there won't be for many years.
    Since I wrote the enclosed letter to Angelino, Netta and I have been talking things over. I think the best solution of the trailer problem will be to join the Automobile Association, and get their advice and help, and a road route. If we can get away from here early next month, the best thing would be to go to Florida until about the middle of April, and then reach Taos about the end of the month. We ought to stay at least a few days at Taos, go up to the ranch and see about the gas tank etc. before actually moving in. I suppose there is somewhere in Taos we could stay? If not, we could camp in the trailer.
    We have some extra baggage and several boxes of books

which can't come in the car. I think the only thing to do is to send them by train. The trouble is that if they are sent off direct from here early in March they would arrive before any of us are there. Have you any agent to whom I could address them? Will you ask Angelino what he thinks the best way of dealing with this difficulty. It has only just occurred to me.

I hope you are having a good time in Hollywood. Do you see Aldous? I sometimes wonder if he is happy in that life out there. I think it would be fun to go to Hollywood on a spree, as you are doing. But to live there! All those rich people must be very tiresome.

How much I look forward to getting away from the East and cities, and living up there in that solitude. One gets awfully degraded with too many people and all these machine-made life.

Ever yours,
Richard

P.S.   I had a copy of my book sent to you at the ranch. Did you get it safely?

c/o Mr J. Lemmon
Jamay Beach
Nokomis
Florida

20 March 1941

Dear Frieda,

Well, here we are, at the end of our first stage on the journey to San Cristóbal. I have been meaning to write you, but I was very tired when I left Washington, and have been idling about here since we arrived. It is a very pleasant place, on the edge of the sea, with a beach of shells and sand where Catherine can play.

We had to alter plans about sending on baggage with our winter clothes and blankets, because the weather suddenly changed, as you know. We were held up in Washington for two days by snowy roads, and even down here it was chilly when we arrived. The last days have been warmer here, and we've been able to bathe, though it's pretty chilly after the Mediterranean! But there are palms and pelicans, and fruit such as oranges and grape-fruit is very cheap. Last week Netta bought from a farm 67 oranges and 21 grape-fruit for 65 cents!

I managed to finish the MS of my anthology two days before we left Washington. It is an enormous affair. The text alone fills 1001 pages of this size, and in addition I had to do an introduction, indexes and a table of contents. Before we leave here, I shall have to do the proofs; and, as publishers are always slow, we shall probably start off a little later than I planned at first—sometime in May instead of April. I think this may be better in some ways, because the mountains will be warmer, though I am longing to see the place.

By the way, you will get a little money from my anthology. I have put in several of Lorenzo's poems—more than by any modern author—and the Viking Press will be writing you for your permission and of course will pay a fee. I think they published some of Lorenzo's later books, didn't they? As I have English editions, I don't know which they published over here. I have been meaning to tell you that recently I have had letters from young men I didn't know ('fan' letters) saying that they were reading Lawrence owing to what I said in the Atlantic, and realised how much he had to say to them.

I look forward so much to seeing you and Angelino I can hardly wait. I have a set of road maps with the route all worked out, and as soon as I get through with those proofs we shall start off.

> All good wishes to you both,
> Richard

El Prado, New Mexico

8 April 1941

Dear Richard,

We are going to have such a nice summer all of us!

We are back at the lower ranch—One day you will go to Hollywood, we have such a good time there! Perhaps you could have 'death of a hero' filmed—

But we shall have so much to talk about—

It is better not to come too soon, it's been a tough winter here—

We will give you a party when you come, already Mabel and Brett, and Myron [Brynig] are wanting to meet you—

Angelino makes pottery and that will interest you—I live as I lived with Lawrence, enjoying my chores and so on; it really is fun getting old—I wonder what Lorenzo would have been like alive and old—But I think only you know, what a tough job it was to be his wife—but worth it, thank God—

Maria Huxley wants to get all her people over from the south of France; there is nothing to eat there—I am also very fond of Gerald Heard and Krishna Murti—

I do so hope you and your wife, which is very important, will like the place—Angelino and I will enjoy the child—

Let us know in time when you come, that we are all spick and span for you—

The snow is melting and it is such a clean, fresh world after all the snow, the road is good all the way, except the last 4 miles, which is awful, but we are getting a grader from the country—

It will do you a lot of good to come from the sea to the mountains—I thought Florida was hot—

You will find everything easy, we have even a radio—But I am so very sick of war and more war. It makes me so angry, if people are too dumb to live, let them die—

But here you are about as far from it as you can be.

It is a lovely sunny day and I think how good it will be to have you for a neighbour—

I suppose England is cross with you as they are is with Aldous for leaving them—

Your Atlantic articles seem to have made much impression.

Get your job over soon and start—

It will be such fun seeing you!

A good journey to you, till you come all good luck!

Frieda

c/o Mr J. Lemmon
Jamay Beach
Nokomis
Florida

14 April 1941

Dear Frieda,

I was very pleased to have your nice letter, and glad to know you and Angelino are happy to be back on the ranch. I have always thought you did so right to go back there. You can imagine how much I look forward to seeing you in the place Lorenzo described so vividly.

Curiously enough, this part of Florida doesn't seem to be so hot. It is sunny, but there always seems to be a cool breeze from the sea, and it is not nearly so hot as places much further north. We intend to come back here in the autumn, and I wish you and Angelino could come and see it. Do you remember that about 1915 some American friend of yours offered to lend you a grape-fruit farm in Florida to live on? A pity you couldn't go, I think you would have liked it. We are too near the sea to grow oranges and grape-fruit, but there are plenty back a couple of miles. We buy oranges and grape-fruit by the half-bushel—about 65 oranges for 35 cents, and 22 grape-fruit for 25 cents.

My proofs are beginning to come in, and I am working on them every day. The trouble is that the book is very long— about 1400 pages it will be, I think—and I have to verify all sorts of tiny little queries about commas and spelling and dates, fiddling work.

We have a bit of trouble. Yesterday (Sunday) we discovered that Catherine has been in contact with a child which has developed measles. I telephoned the doctor at the Medical Centre (about four miles from here) and he is getting some serum from Tampa. If we can get her inoculated to-day, there is a good chance she may escape it or at any rate only have it mildly. But if she does get it, we shall be held up for some weeks. It makes me so cross because Catherine was so well and happy, and the parents knew the other child had been exposed to measles contagion, but didn't tell us.

I have just heard that Norman has escaped from France to Portugal, and is staying at a place near Ponte da Lima. I have been there. It is in Northern Portugal, and very beautiful country, rather like Tuscany, with piney hills and vineyards and olives and wheat and rather lovely old villages. Robin Douglas [Son of Norman] wants me to try to persuade Norman to come here. But I have a feeling he wouldn't like America, and that Portugal will please him. It is like Italy must have been 70 or 80 years ago, peasants all in lovely costumes, real folk music and dancing, and living very cheap. The British Government allows Norman only $34 dollars a month from his investments in England, but he ought to be able just to live on that in Portugal, and he certainly couldn't live on it in America.

Charles Prentice (who you remember him—Chatto) writes me that he hears Pino is somewhere in South America. But Pino hasn't written to any of his friends in England for ages. I wish I knew what has happened to him. After all his waiting and dangling after Reggie, the money hasn't done him much good unless he was able to get it out of England in time. Perhaps he did. I hope so, for otherwise I'm afraid it will be confiscated.

So far as I know, I have not been criticised [for pacifism] in England as Aldous has. The fact that I was in the last war for nearly three years seems to make the difference. At any rate, I still get press cuttings, and there have been no newspaper attacks on me. It seems very absurd to criticise Aldous. He is over military age, and all he could do would be to write propaganda and talk it over the radio like Jack Priestley, and I feel sure he wouldn't do such a thing. It is just little people who are jealous of Aldous's great gifts and his success.

I though a lot about Lorenzo in March—he has been dead eleven years—and re-read some of his books. I still love the travel ones, Sea and Sardinia, Twilight in Italy, Mornings in Mexico, Kangaroo. The English ones seem very far away now, but there are beautiful things in them. If he had lived he still wouldn't be old. 56 this September. How well he felt that this collapse was bound to come—you remember he talked of it at Scandicci and Port Cros. How long will it be before America is involved? Not long, I fancy.

It was very difficult to choose from Lorenzo's poems for the anthology. I realised this when I made that Selected Edition of his poems for Heinemann about seven years ago. It is the whole collection which is so impressive, the continuous revealing of experience and personality. But they don't make museum pieces, which is what an anthology is. ~~But~~ I put in the Ship of Death, but even that is much more vivid when you come on it after reading all the others than it is by itself . . .

I'll let you know well ahead of time when we are starting. I imagine the journey will take about 10 days, as we have to give Catherine rests, although she is marvellous on these long car journeys. On the 1100 miles from Washington here she wasn't once fretful, and spent a lot of time lying on a mattress on ~~the~~ top of the baggage looking out the back window. She was terrifically excited by the big mules in North and South Carolina, and wanted to have one.

All good wishes to you both, and thanks to Angelino for his saluti.

> Ever yours,
> Richard

> c/o Mr J. Lemmon
> Jamay Beach
> Nokomis, Fla.

> 12 May 1941

Dear Frieda,

I am getting through the work well, practically all done now, except for one set of proofs.

There are three things I'd like to know if possible before we leave.

(1) Can you arrange for me to cash cheques in Taos? Otherwise I must get some sort of Letter of Credit from my New York Bank.

(2) Is there a good toy shop in Taos? Catherine has her third birthday on July 6th, and we want to make it a nice one since it will really be the first she is able to appreciate. If we can't get toys in Taos, we must get some here and bring along.

(3) What address should I give for parcels and letters and in case I need to send a suit-case or two ahead?

It will be just two weeks from to-day that we start out! It is <u>very</u> exciting.

> Ever yours,
> Richard

Jamay Beach
Nokomis, Fla.

1 August 1941

Dearest Frieda,

We made a rapid and pleasant return journey, though we were a little tired at the end. I didn't dare attempt any of the unpaved roads after the rain, so we went direct to Santa Fe, and then by Route 41 to the main road from California to Texas. That Route 41 was almost deserted and ran through very fine country. On the first night we stopped at Clarendon, Texas, about 50 miles beyond Amarillo, and on Saturday crossed Texas and stopped at Marshall, Texas, close to the Louisiana border. On Sunday we crossed Louisiana and most of Mississippi and stayed at Pascagoula, and by Monday morning we were in Florida. The coast drive from Pensacola to Apalachicola is one of the loveliest I have ever seen— brilliant white sands with blue sea and sky, miles of uninhabited coast, and huge long bridges connecting the islands. Tallahassee looked very nice with its white colonial houses under great shady live oaks hung with Spanish moss. Further south we stopped at Rainbow Springs, where they take you out on the crystal clear lake in a boat with underwater port-holes, and you see multitudes of fish and turtles and water weeds which at a certain angle are fringed with the rainbow colours. On Tuesday we had lunch in Sarasota, did our week's shopping, and arrived back here in time for an afternoon wa bathe. It is not oppressively hot here, and there is a ceaseless cool breeze from the sea which blows through the cottage.

The pain in Netta's lung suddenly disappeared when we got a little below Albuquerque, but to my alarm it returned the day after we reached sea level. It was rather bad on Tuesday and Wednesday, but began to fade on Thursday, and to-day has practically gone. I hope and believe it will now stay away, but if it returns we shall of course have to start the dreary business of doctors. Catherine is very well and enjoys her sea bathing and running about the place, though she regrets Anita and the piggy. 'Where's Angie?' she asks about milking time. And in the morning: 'Shall we go and see Frieda?' To console her we say you and Angie will come and see her here one of these days.

I am sending to Angie the Mondadori Un Vero Paradiso and Le Donne devono lavorare, and including copies of Seven Against Reeves and Rejected Guest for you and a little pamphlet [on Aldington] by Dr C. P. Snow, a Cambridge scientist who is interested in literature. I think the Viking will probably send you a copy of the anthology as Lorenzo's poems are in it, but if they don't I will. To my annoyance I find I have only one copy of Heldentod and one of Tutti gli uomini sono nemici, and haven't duplicates to send you.

I wish you had told me sooner that you would have liked some of the butterflies and moths. I could easily have left you a box. They travelled all the way here without the slightest damage, so that I think when I have time to go over the collection I will try to pick out and classify for you a set of the Kiowa Ranch butterflies. If they are very firmly pinned in and packed with plenty of shavings I think they ought to go through the post all right. There are no new shells on the beach, as the sea is so calm all summer; but after the autumn storms there'll be plenty. We will collect a set for you. But it would be ever so much better if you and Angie would come and get them! The place is wonderfully peaceful, as there is nobody here at all except the owner and his parents who don't bother us in the least.

We are still in the process of unpacking, and my hut is still half filled with some of the stuff we left here and the books and suit cases from San Cristóbal. I don't know why it takes such a time to get one's miserable little possessions in order, but it does. However, we shall gradually get straightened out. I have had one last-minute (and totally unimportant) query from the Viking since I got back, but nothing else thank goodness!

I think of you both very often and of the now famous ranch which I am so glad to have seen. It is a beautiful place, and I am so sorry that we got upset by the altitude. You were both so good to us and so sweet with Catherine—I don't know how to thank you. I do wish you could manage to come here for a stay sometime. It is so different, but with a quality of its own. Just now the seaward edge of the island is fringed with a lovely tall grass, nearly as big as pampas grass though more elegant; and all day the heads bend and sway in the sea breeze. I wish I could send you a bunch of them.

Netta joins me in love to you both.

Richard

Marianna, Fla.

27 September 1941

Dearest Frieda,

We did 400 miles yesterday and may be with you sooner than we expected.

I have sent 4 packages of books by mail addressed to Kiowa Ranch and 3 suit-cases and 1 light box to Autonito, Colorado. The railway people at Venice, Fla. said Autonito was the head of the railway. Hope these won't bother you. We shall make the best speed possible.

Ever yours
Richard

Jamay Beach
Nokomis, Fla.

31 December 1941

Dearest Frieda,

I have indeed been very remiss about writing, but I was so tired after that anthology that I hated even to write a letter. And now for some weeks I have been trying to get together material for another book. And that is not easy. It is enough to have experienced two world wars without having to write books as well.

You are very wise to stay in Taos, where you are among friends. I feel quite sure that you and Angie will not be molested if you just keep quiet and go about your own lives as usual. There has been no scare here at all, though we have a practice blackout this week.

It is simply beautiful down here now—lovely sunny days with a cool or warm breeze and a bathe every afternoon. The winter visitors are beginning to arrive, and Catherine now has other children to play with. So what with the Christmas tree and present from Santa Claus and new friends, she is in a blissful state.

I did not read Aldous's book, but I intend to do so speedily. He is almost the only living author whose every book I want to read.

The anthology was attacked by several minor poets who also happened to be reviewers, but it has survived and has been selling better and better. The Literary Guild took 60,000 copies, and I believe that over 15,000 of the ordinary edition have already gone. People sent it out as a Christmas present, and one university sent an order for 80 copies.

Otherwise life goes on quietly with very little to report. I hear Norman and Pino are still in Portugal with Carletto, and that once more Pino has a fegato [liver trouble]. Norman had some difficulty in getting an extension of his permis de sejour, but triumphed in the end. It must seem a queer world to him with his diplomatic passport signed by Queen Victoria! But no doubt he contrives to enjoy himself.

We are very fortunate to be in America. Those people who took refuge in 'idyllic islands' in the Pacific made a bad blunder.

I hope all goes well with you and that you'll write when you have time.

Ever affectionately,
Richard

Port Isabel
Texas

7 January 1948

Dear Richard,

Just got your letter! Deep inside me I rejoice for Lawrence a million! Not that I despise the shekels either, I don't. But I am sure people are fed up to the teeth with war and hate and murder and politics—They need the human thing Lawrence has to give! Wouldn't he be happy that at least one of his fellow-travellers is interested in his output—

Yes, I know about Mondadori—I believe the books are selling, people seem to want books again. Yes, Viking wants to buy some of the English sheets.

Yes, America can't seem to get ahead with L—I felt a resistance and you are right it's the Jews—That's why there has never been a movie. I don't want to go to New York, it's also better, those people don't like me and I just don't understand what makes them tick—Do you know anything about ~~my~~ Editions des ~~Deux~~ Rives in Paris? If I told you all my publishing troubles you would feel sorry for me—

I have Alan Collins of Curtis Brown, 347 Madison Avenue, New York, 17 for agent, but he doesn't do much—

Glad the biography moves—

Yours
Frieda

I thank you—Richard!

I nearly forgot: My sister Johanna flew from Vienna—She is splendidly so happy to be here and she has the 'grand manner' so rare! I am having such fun with her! What a hell of a time she had!

[Ironic remark about Jews, because Lawrence's U.S. publishers and boosters were Jewish.—eds]

El Prado
Taos
New Mexico

16 October 1948

Dear Richard,

I hope you will write a frightfully good book.

Lately I have seen Lorenzo in a new light. I see him in the tradition of the St. Augustine (his confessions) even of Francis of Assisi with Lorenzo's almost uncanny love for animals and plants. I could never see Lawrence in line with english novelists, it is something different.

I hope you see what I mean, he is so interesting from this angle.

When I read in the St. Augustine confessions 'O Lord help me to perceive thee, Help me to perceive myself. For understanding thee, I will know about myself', etc——Don't you agree that Lawrence is a descendant of these men?

You would know more about them than I do—

As to the Café Royal incident, I heard it from Katherine very much as it is in 'Women in Love'. I remember the letter—you remember Heseltine had a 'white love', Juliette, afterwards Julian Huxley's wife and a dark love Puma who was with us in Cornwall going to have a child by Heseltine— There were some skirmishes there then—I can't remember who read the letter, I know that Russian was there, Bob Nichols was in the war, wasn't he? I don't believe Michael Arlen was there—Anyhow Heseltine must have shown that letter—He was either angelic or the other thing and blew hot and cold—

I know you loved Lawrence, but I hope you can detach yourself enough from the Lawrence you knew, to look behind the surface and see the man in his full significance—I give you my permission to use my book and so does Brett, but Mabel wants you to write to her——

Good luck to the enterprise,

Yours ever,
Frieda

Port Isabel
Texas

20 November 1948

Dear Richard,

I am here where I bought a little house right on the gulf—Now to your questions—My mother's name was Anna Marquier, of French descent. Onkel Ferdinand was an uncle, he also found a means to reopen the Comstock Lode,—Yes the Richthofens came from Silesia and all their estates are gone now—I think Cooley [in Lawrence's *Kangaroo*] was a mixture of Dr Eder and Kot [S. S. Koteliansky]—No Lorenzo never went to political meetings—Jack and Victoria something like them were on the boat—No, the [?spy] story did not happen. About the only paper Lawrence read was the Sydney Bulletin.

The story of Mss and books is a long, long 'tail' of woe—Pollinger sent me a whole catalogue of L's books and my own Mss, a bookseller in Scotland and I don't know his name, the catalogue is in Taos (Yes I found the catalogue—Melvin, 156 St. John's Road, Edinburgh 12). Send for the catalogue and you will see—I left a trunk with Orioli and he I suppose left all to Norman Douglas—And the Mss of my book 'Not I but the wind' is there for sale for 75£—!! How it got away from me I can't imagine!—Medley is looking into it—Yes, I suppose the Eliot clique are enemies. Lawrence must have some enemies in America too, but I don't know who they are—But there is also a revival here among the young—I wish you could look at all the stuff of his I have!

I read Rainbow and Women in Love again and got puffed up—It's me, It's me, so much is me!—But then I thought, no he sensed it, he turned it into art and I subsided again—

Wasn't Katherine [Mansfield] brave! It shows how people imagine things! I so distinctly see that letter with 'flux of corruption' in it! There you are! And Miriam [Jessie Chambers, the Miriam of *Sons and Lovers*] dead!

Good luck to your work

Ever yours
Frieda

You know that in a book [*Memoirs of a Bookseller*], Orioli is mean about L—That was a shock! influenced by Douglas, who hated L—

Laguna Vista
Port Isabel
Texas

2 January 1949

Dear Richard,

Thank you for your good long letter—It is a great satisfaction to me, that you fight so hard for Lorenzo's work—In a way I was sorry those Lawrence–Russell letters were published—I never thought Russell would want them published. They do not add to either L's or Russell's stature, they were neither of them practical politicians.—I am sure Harry Moore asked Frere's permission. I had a letter that Viking will take some of the Penguin books.

Achsah Brewster is dead. Earl wrote to me last about 3 years ago from a convent in India. 'Almora' but I have not the right address—I fear Earl may be dead too—

Yes, Garda was important for L—Italy was a happy revelation for him—Yes, I know how much I meant to him, a hell of a lot, but one does not want to blow one's own trumpet

and has one's 'pudeur' about those things. You remember
yourself how jealous he was, at Port-Cros, though he was fond
of you, as you know! We quarrelled a lot, but that was because
the connection was so deep—Not a sort of love affair, it was
more: it was an infinite joy of living and sharing all that life
had to offer—You know, Richard, I think he was so much
more than an english novelist, a teller of stories; he was a
visionary, a new way of life—a sort of religion, I think sex was
the only thing that had not been approached religiously and
he did it. After all it's the root of all being. People go on
superficialising him and misunderstanding him! That's that!
damn it!

My sister Johanna (called Nusch) came yesterday from
Vienna—She has guts but the stories she tells about all the
pettifogging that goes on and the misery are so maddening—I
think people go on by sheer irritation—And the Russians
wash their feet in the toilet!!

I love it here! Yes, the birds! O those birds, the flights of
white geese in a snakeline and we eat duck that Angie gets and
fish from the fishermen and oysters and shrimp and boats
from Hawaii with bananas, great trees for a dollar a
pineapple—The richness of this valley is unbelievable—
Nusch gasps at the shops here! Catherine [Aldington] 10! I
can't believe it! Is she as charming as ever? I have this little nice
house here on the gulf, but go back to Taos in April. Angie
loves it here! Don't forget that Frere loves and admires you
very much, I think you can do what you like with him—I hope
this publishing plan comes off—I liked your friend's face—
Aldous and Maria were happy in Rome—but wanted to come
back. I am always in trouble about something or other of L's!

I also meant to do what I can, that he is read and he is read
all over the world, but America and England are still superior
and sniffy about him! Well, it takes time—One has to take the
long view!

I am trying to write myself, but go so slowly!

Yes, I know they think I was 'bad' for L! From their narrow
point of view I was! They would have liked him to be a tame,
little writer ~~of~~ about nice, well behaved little people! Pah!

Good luck to you!

Ever yours
Frieda

Well, dear Richard I am still here and I have no plans to go—I
like America and I am happy—I would not know how to cope
with that crazy and old Europe. They should learn something
from two wars—but they go on in the same old fashion. <u>Love
to all of you</u>, <u>Angie</u>.

Port Isabel
Texas

21 March 1949
(beginning of spring)

Dear Richard,

It is really very thrilling, all those Lawrence books! Of
course from a money point of view it isn't so very hot but
infinitely satisfactory for all that! No, I mean yes and no,
Lawrence is not forgotten, much goes on about him at
Universities, but somehow officially they try to ignore him,
but they don't succeed—you know the longer it takes for him
to be established finally the better it is! Think what Compton
Mackenzie was and Galsworthy and lots of others—That
[T. S.] Eliot for instance is quite good as a sort of professor, but
his writing is like decorating skeletons, there is no life in
his writing, no flesh and blood and bones, nor the breath of
life.

. . . I see <u>your</u> name in the New York Times occasionally! I
hope you don't get sick and tired of all that hard work!

This is a story you might use! Lawrence had written
'Phantasia' [Fantasia] and a letter came from a young english
doctor and Lawrence was pleased with the letter, L wrote the
doctor and there came a letter back; 'I am ~~really~~ very embar-
rassed; what I did was really making fun of your book'—

What a very good-looking man your friend Kershaw is and
strangely he looks so much like you, when we knew you first.

It is fun having my sister with me and I realise what a lot it
means to belong to a family of unusual men, it means a lot—I
suffered tortures of shame about the Nazis being german, but
many of the members of the family were anti-nazi and did all
they could. The trouble was they did not take Hitler seriously
till it was too late—

We go back to Taos on the 20th of April—

I wish I could help you more, it is a big job you are doing—

I think Pollinger will go through now with contracts. He has been a wonderful agent really and knows all about L's work!

All good luck
Frieda

Port Isabel
Texas

5 April 1949

Dear Richard,

No, it's nice of you to let me share your work with you, as it were— I wish I could be more help—

I am glad you are where you are, it sounds good, I am just reading Montaigne again, what a sane and sound and lovable man he is!

England, there seems something, almost sadistic in those [Sir Stafford] Crippses! I am not only amused at your . . . story, I am terribly pleased. He is so sinfully dull and dumb and a smart Alec; his book on english poets, how he writes about Yeats makes one want to hit him! Yes, those war years were terrible for Lawrence, he was not quite sane at times, as you say. A few times I was really scared of him, except for the last bit of me—You also know (between you and me) in his bewilderment he had a passionate attachment for a cornish farmer, but of course it was a failure—I suppose you don't mention that or <u>should you</u>? There is one poem about the man, but I only remember the word 'mowie' [?] in it.

I have had a letter from a Prof. Wm. White in Detroit, he has made a bibliography of Lorenzo or rather books and essays on him—600 and more! Your name is there twice: I. in the 'Inselschiff'. 1932. II Last Poems Florence 32 and Viking 33 and William Heinemann 35.

To-day I had a letter from a Hindu who does his M.A. thesis on Lorenzo—And another clever one who is unhappy under . . .! I think you are right about 'The man who died'. I also think the Magnus is very good. [The late Maurice Magnus, for whose book on the Foreign Legion (1934) Lawrence wrote a long introduction, whose portrait of Magnus, whom he had know in Italy and Malta, was one of Lawrence's finest pieces of writing.] Why Cecil Grey is so bitter about Lawrence is rather strange, I remember things in his book [*Musical Chairs*] that weren't true. Because I am sure Lawrence was right about Heseltine—We had his 'dark love' Puma staying with us at Zennor [Cornwall]—About Murry, well Murry is like that. I think one of the chief points about Lawrence is that he was always aware of the elemental, the unpredictable in people, as Montaigne says: 'We are all wind. And even the wind more wisely than we, loves to make a noise and move about, and is content with its own functions, without wishing for stability and solidity, qualities that do not belong to it'—Don't work too hard!

You would like my sister Nusch! All she had is confiscated! I hope she can stay, but it is doubtful! We all send you our best greetings to you all. If you have a photograph to spare of Catha, do send it please, we would so like to see what she is like now!

We go back to Taos on the 20th of April!

The best of luck!

Frieda

I believe L suffered so much in the war, because he saw his adored England not come up to 'his scratch'; then being a fighter and not believing in that war, wanting the greatness of war, 'The Love of Comrades', that no woman can give—

El Prado

12 October 1949

Dear Richard,

Your enthusiastic letter made me very happy. Such wonderful news! Send me your book as soon as it is ready; I want to read it so much—You soaked yourself in Lawrence and the splendid result is that you are not fed up with him! It is a fine thing you have done! Yes, it is too bad Lawrence cannot be got in America—

They are making a film of 'You Touched Me'. I had such a polite letter from a japanese publisher wanting to publish Lawrence promising a roll of real japanese silk!!

All this fame is almost too much! I was 70! but am well, I am thankful to say.

I like your selection of the essays. Yes, I wish you could have published the Norman [Douglas] letter. Can't you shove it in somewhere or quote from it?

I am grateful to be alive, that I at least have the fun of seeing the result of L's work—and I am grateful to you who have been so initial in this rebirth. I suppose it was also a need in you to write his life as you saw it, in a way it is your own fight too—

It is very nice to have my sister here and on the whole we have a very good time, lots of people and many want to have your news—I also hope you get something out of all your hard work! I mean spondulicks!

Love to you all
We will drink to the venture!

Yours ever
Frieda

Your address is pretty!

31 October 1949

Dear Richard,

I am doing my best—But so many photographs have gone to Mondadori, the last bunch, but I am having reprints made of the ranch ones, found the negatives—Will send to Charles Duell—I found an awfully nice <u>unpublished</u> photo of L's that they must put in—Lorenzo with a white cat, called Miss Wemyss—I agree you should have photographs of all the parts of his life.

Saw Bynner yesterday who has also written on L and me in Mexico, but that will be different, only a slice—

I want to help all I can, naturally—Also I want to give you an Mss—you certainly ought to have one—

Of course you must <u>not</u> pay for photographs—

Ever yours
Frieda

Yes, from the early days they wanted Lawrence to remain a tame little english writer!

Port Isabel
Texas

29 November 1949

Dear Richard,

We were on the move, that's why I was so long in answering. Walter Goodwin the nice young man who is at Duell's [Duell, Sloan and Pearce, New York publishers of Aldington's biography of D. H. Lawrence] wrote me very enthusiastically about your book—I sent him the photos; that book may do a lot for Lawrence over here—They are doing a broadcast play here of 'Sons and Lovers'.

I would love having a set of your galleys from Duell. The nice 'Penguin' sent me proofs too, thank you for asking them—It is nice to have them—Tennessee Williams wrote a sort of a last act about L and Brett and me, good in a way, but too much hate between the sexes—

If you were 'tender' towards me, I am not ashamed—Didn't they say enough nasty things about me? God! but I am grateful!! I want very much to give you a Lorenzo Mss! Have you an idea what you would like, tell me—Lots are also stolen and lost and sold—So I may not have the one you want, say several—That is a loss, your letters—from all these people—It is so warm and bright, the fishermen, Mexicans, just brought some oysters. My sister Nusch is on the shore below—Hardly any people, a relief—The Penguin are ready in March—I am thrilled. Maybe [William] Dieterle will buy Lady C for the films—But what will they make of it—

Aldous wrote: 'I am writing. When Gibbon took the 4th volume to Lord X the lord said: What Mr Gibbon another damn book! Scribble, scribble all the time.'

What an unsettled world it is! The young roaming around, lost! One has to hang on hard to one's bit of whole inside—

Yours ever,
Frieda

Port Isabel
Texas

4 December 1949

Dear Richard,

Is this a true nature butterfly or a fancy one? I have to laugh when you get furious like Lorenzo about people like [publisher Walter] Goodwin, he <u>means</u> well though—

Now it will make you cross again because Pollinger wrote that the censor (british) has refused to give permission to have a film made with the title 'Lady Chatterley's Lover'. Dieterle wanted Lady C—O dreary world—You also know that Mondadori is doing all of L's books—

I liked the photo of L with the cat so much—aware of the cat but not sentimental—Mondadori had some photos too, never sent them back—Here is a letter from L to Nusch's husband, <u>Emil Krug</u>, not published. Send it back to her, please—here—

Now about the pictures, that is too bad of me—I did not read it properly—Of course I have no pictures here—I am so glad to have the Penguins.

Millions of ducks, I love the way they fly! My sister Nusch is with us! She is fun!

Now I hope the Duell send me your book so that will be something.

Love from A and Frieda

I met a great admirer of yours the other day!

Taos
New Mexico

Easter Sunday
[13 April] 1950

Dear Richard,

There I have been waiting for your book every day, Walter Goodwin promised to send it, it hasn't come yet! You must have thought it queer I hadn't written! The minute it comes I will read it and tell you! I got the little pamphlet with the Penguins, I liked that enormously— that L. was a heretic is so right!

You must be glad it is behind you—I like the Penguin books

too—There they are! I am looking anxiously in the New York Times for a review of your book—and your own too! My good news is: They sent me a french play of Lady C—excellent, I thought, delicate and alive—done by Gaston Bonhuer and Philippe de Rothschild! Do you know about them? I don't—

Your letters are always full of interest—

I send you this by Harry Moore—

Brett is in Jamaica with Millicent Rogers—

Taos grows—We have just come back from Port Isabel, a storm today!

I wrote to Frere—I agree, books of the months are not up your and L's alley.

So I am waiting impatiently for your book—

It's strange, all sorts of unexpected people have read Lady C— colonels and generals—So my best wishes go out for the 'books'—

Love to you all. Is Netta back? You will have to see that french play!

Frieda

I am asking Pollinger for the book on you!

El Prado
Taos

[ante 26 April 1950]

Dear Richard,

At long last I have read the book [*Portrait of a Genius, But...*]—It was a strange experience—I forgot that it was about Lawrence and read it like Plutarch's lives and about me like another person. Many things, as our wills clashing, I had not really grasped, but it's true—I am glad you were nice about Aldous, but you did not say enough, how patient and kind you were and when Hilda took us in at that bad moment you had something to do with it too—you know how scared everybody was of us! I think I took it all too lightly and never realised how serious it all was! My love for him was strange too he was a sort of new element for me and though he bullied me, I also felt free to be myself and I never told him any lies, it wouldn't have been any use, he knew about me anyhow—Yes, you are kind to me in your book. But I think English women especially will not ever like me—I could go on a long time talking to you and telling you more things like at the Fontana Vecchia when he was worked up and finally had his hands on my throat and said fiercely: 'I am the master, I am the master'! and I said in astonishment: 'Is that all? I don't care, you can be the master as much as you like'. And then he was astonished allright. Well, we are strange creatures and more than 'meets the eye'.

All good luck to the books, yours and L's! That Philippe de Rothschild is coming next week—You'll have to see the play in Paris! Have you ever written about Napoleon? Do you remember how thrilled I was about the trumpeter who fainted?

Well all my gratitude for the book.

I will get the book on you from Pollinger—

I had to laugh in many places!

Yours ever
Frieda

El Prado
New Mexico

2 May 1950

Dear Richard

When you get this letter I hope you are all well again. When I got your letters of the last few months I knew you were working so very hard, too hard—Such exacting intense work—No wonder you were worn out—You sent me an avalanche of reviews—It surely is what's called success—I even doubt if Winston Churchill (20 years dead) will get such a reception! So there we are! It's terribly nice of you to say they would treat me like a queen, I would be such a bad queen! And you know that deep down I feel so sure because of L—They had a nice 'Sons and Lovers' on N.B.C., respectful! And again I felt what I meant to L—(I tell you this I hope in all modesty, because it isn't my <u>merit</u>, it just happened. When his mother was dead, and you know Miriam [Jessie Chambers] meant a lot to him intellectually and culturally, humanly she could not, she was by nature a bluestocking—he was in and was at the end of his tether—Long hours we talked over, I could give him new life!

Did you send a book to Aldous?

'Sons and Lovers', there are even bits that I wrote like how the mother felt and so on—I don't need anymore—I am allright. Maybe when you are an old man, you will ~~right~~ write a critical book on L and his inner development—I feel it vaguely—But I know there is a logic or a consequence in it—you are a writer, a real one and I can see how much of your strength you put in that book—at the right moment too—I wrote something to the 'Times'—Smart Alec! Wouldn't I be more than furious at the state England is in? Bad cheap doctoring is all I can see; drowned in their 'sweat and blood and tears' so superiorly!! Hilda, how is she? I shall always be grateful to her, she wasn't 'small beer' anyhow, what a strange marriage of yours that must have been! Anyhow what do we know about each others relationships always a mystery!

I hope you get some money for all this! I got finally your american edition, it looks very nice! I don't know which I like better—You were right not to see Bynner under the circumstances! A young friend wrote from Rome, lots of books there too! So write that you are well!

F——

El Prado

4 May 1950

Dear Richard,

More clippings! My sister read your book and liked it so very much, read it all night—I have heard nothing but praise! Stephen Spender also—I hope by now you are well—Hope you can take a rest now—I pinch myself and say: 'You are famous too!' but what does it really mean? I don't think I shall ever know. Then I remember on the day Lawrence died I read in the 'Daily Mail': It is a strange fact that of these two writers of pornography James Joyce and D.H.L.—one is blind and the other is dying of consumption. That was the funeral oration of a great nation to one of its sons.—

I have a disease called 'Vikingitis' that attacks me occasionally—In now 20 years they have produced a 'Portable

D.H.L.' —mangy little books, a 'Mark Twain' one too and others—a long tale of woe—I seem helpless—I have tried— They are dogs in the manger. Is it the Jewish element that suppresses him? Do you remember in Port-Cros you did so much for L and you say not a word in your book. I at the time was so grateful for your friendship and the life you gave me, with L so ill—When you yourself were in one of those difficult moments of your life—a lot is happening all the time, almost too much for me now—I had to pay 11,000 dollars back income tax—I hope it is not right. It is snowing—I hope it's the last—A man, Beaumont Wadsworth, sent me L's first story, that he unearthed from the Nottingham Guardian—Isn't it strange, the reviews goes with L as far as 'Sons and Lovers', then their interest dies—The english seem to have stood still for the last twenty years—When I think how impressed I was with the England I saw at 15! So grand, so sure and proud! I would not be impressed now I fear! I wonder if Brett and Netta met in Jamaica—Brett is there with Millicent Rogers—I expect Rothschild about the french play of Lady C—You must see it—

Ever,
Frieda

22 May 1950

Dear Richard,

Thank you for telling me all that happens!

Harry Moore wrote me he liked your book—This is the first review I saw here—So I send it you quickly—

Anyhow we laugh,—it is really amusing—One's enemies fall by the way in the long run—

I think it is only splendid of Frere to do what he can, when he believes in a man—

Baron Philippe de Rothschild of Avenue d'Iena Paris (16) came, a very human fellow, I want you to know him and you must see the Lady C play—he is a dynamo, has wine near Bordeaux—

Montgomery Clift has bought 'you touched me'—It is really exciting this Lawrence revival—I get a swelled head—aren't you really pleased at the effect you have had?

You never know what Murry might say—

Just a word to get this to you—
Hope you are well again

Frieda

['You Touched Me' was a story later dramatised by Tennessee Williams and produced on Broadway in 1945, starring Clift and Edmund Gwenn. The story Clift bought was 'The Fox', in which he never played. — eds]

El Prado

27 May 1950

Dear Richard,

You seem to have unleashed a whirlwind with your very human book! The same raging as 20 years ago—Did you have any idea it would still be such a fight? It is more than Lawrence and you, it's the fight, the <u>good</u> fight! No wonder it takes it out of you, it's like lifting a tombstone—I am not surprised they didn't print my letter, I said a man is supposed to be judged by his peers!—It always was a middleclass paper that Times—Strange at the same time the Prince [sic] of Windsor's 'Memoirs' in Life appear—His fight too—I have a hunch your book might sell better in America—

You are right not to write any more to the press. Your book stands. You are absolutely right: L's life and writing were one and he himself thought his living more important that his writing. Your book on L has in a way the simplicity of Montaigne—I don't know why I feel that—Poor Hilda [H.D.]! people do go off the hooks of reality—But the english now know that you have taken your stand—that takes some courage, lots of it—In the end you will feel stronger than ever! I am glad you have your friend Alister and Netta and the child! Now take it easy and relax! (as they say here!)

My head is not really swelled but so surprised! How you have got under their skin or rather rhinoceros hide! If the 'badly printed Penguins' don't smell of envy, I don't know whatever did!

A letter went to you this morning!

As ever
Your old friend
F

Box 201
Port Isabel
Texas

29 March 1954

Dear Richard,

Of course I swallowed your 'Pinorman' like a raw oyster. You made it all alive again. You give this wonderful bit of living, unique, never to be repeated. I laugh when I think what ordinary people will make of it.

You treat Pino with special tenderness. I am glad. How good he was, when Lawrence was so ill and I sent for him, and at once he came, bringing Dr Giglioli mostly. Then came the bitter blow of his meanness. I am sure it was Norman. I don't think Lawrence ever knew how much Norman hated him.

I knew Norman earlier than you when he still had his full diabolic splendor, that could not have friends only slaves. But you are fair to him, you could have presented an ogre feeding on small boys. He saw himself as that finished article the 'perfect gentleman', but did not seek the society of other perfect gentlemen, but wild, unsophisticated urchins, that freshened up his weary soul.

I do hope Pino did not die in misery and loneliness. But somehow Pino would always find somebody to be good to him, Pino did not write anything nasty about me. I wonder why?

What a lie when Norman says the peasants did not like L. at the Mirenda. They did very much. In their own way they knew he was somebody. Not in a 'frere et cochon' way (as my father would say) but very real. I <u>love</u> it when you say: 'If Pino said that, I won't speak to him again, either in heaven or hell'.

That you defend L. like a cat her kittens is wonderful but surely fair! I don't think L. was envious, you cannot be, when you are as much 'yourself' as L. was!

Richard, now I say: mea culpa. I had forgotten that you got Frere to take L's books. Ingratitude, but now I will remember—and be grateful!

Good luck to 'Pinorman'. I am glad it was written and how it was written!

Ever yours,
Frieda

Had Douglas read Gregorovius?

El Prado
New Mexico

5 April 1954

Dear Richard,

Thank you for your last letter, telling so much. I hope you have got mine via Frere with my enthusiasm for 'Pinorman'. You gave the atmosphere so beautifully. It ought to be a success. But you know, Richard, I am really surprised that 'they' have not attacked Frere yet, he is so staunch in his defense of the right things. But I feel Lawrence is so firmly established, they can't do much. That magistrate who called Lady C rubbish, is the kind that would call anything beyond a kippered herring rubbish. No, I can't say any more on the B.B.C. because the tape has gone. Do you remember the story of Pino about Reggie [Turner], practising on his new telephone? Do you remember Reggie's story about Aubrey Beardsley? Reggie found him with a long face in front of a looking glass. When Reggie asked 'What are you doing'? Aubrey said: 'That's what I shall look like when I am dead.' I suppose Pino had more or less gone to pieces, that he could be so weak. Maybe N even did it without Pino's knowledge. Some bold publisher is trying over here to publish an unexpurgated Lady C. Yes, I answered Bertie, more 'in sorrow than in anger' in a magazine, now I forget its name. And in Houston, Texas a young schoolteacher was dismissed because he gave his students L to read, and Lawrence is a 'communist' in Houston. The paper published my protest! I think your phrase: 'who would have thought the old men had so much hate in them', squashes them. That poor Bertie must have turned into a sourpuss! I hate Coca Cola! Catha must be a great source of interest and life to you. Tell me how old she is, when you write again—The drive from Port Isabel here was very nice, masses of flowers along the road and young green on the woods till we got near Lubbock and then it was terrible, nothing but sand, the farmhouses forsaken, no chickens at the back, no sign of life. It's their own stupidity, they pulled up every tree and there is nothing to protect those big fields! It makes me so mad when people don't use their wits.

It will please you to know how L. is alive among the young;

but there is, I feel, a definite attempt to keep him under, but it can't be done, I say triumphantly to myself.

Love to you and Cathy, from Angie too—
    Frieda

A man called Angell wants to make a film of Lady C—

El Prado
Taos
New Mexico

[27] May [1954]

Monty wrote Prof Weekley died!

Dear Richard,
    Aren't you amused how you got under their concrete skins? Oh they are mad! 'A hyena that doesn't laugh!' It makes me laugh! You take the long, long view and laugh too! He contradicts himself: he writes: 'Norman is far from being the only person etc'—and then—'I cannot see Lord Russell as a brazier of vindictive hate'. It is passionate hate from Bertie. Their small beer vanities and egos! I am glad I knew another England! How can Churchill be a great leader if under him the greatest nation on earth became a second-rate one. Do you remember 'Bundles for Britain?'
    I tell you this story about Douglas. I did not want to tell you, it's so ugly. At Florence with Pino he told me: 'I have a boy of fourteen and I prefer them younger, would you like to take him over?' I believe I said: 'I have children of my own'. He would not have said that to me, if L. had been alive. But it finished me with Norman. I am so anxious to read the Colonel Lawrence—I read the 'Lawrence of Arabia' and my impression was of a strange unreality and I remember nothing—I am glad you are not in England and you have wonderful friends, thank the Lord for that.
    There is so much activity around L here!
    I remember when L stayed with Bertie [Bertrand Russell] at Cambridge and came back, he had had a shock. When he told me about me it, he acted for me how after dinner they walked

round the room the other professors with their hands on their backs and discussed the Balkans in a professional way and they knew really nothing, L said. But he was bitter about their deadness. I am glad you sent my Time and Tide to Frere. I hope you noticed I tried to be very sober.

Don't let them hurt you, they are so small and you can't make them bigger.

Love to you and Catha, she is having a good time!

Greetings from Angie, he is interested too—

Frieda

'Ma Le mi toccana ~~al~~ nel mio debole divento una vi-vipera' is a song of A's!

That Times wasn't criticism but abuse, so he was another who hated L—and never had the guts to say so while L was alive! Three cheers!

But isn't it mysterious that they defend with such ferocity a man who has been through all the sordidness of trials, who was not allowed to live in England? I can't make out the meaning or what lies behind it.

Les Rosiers
Ancien chemin de Castelnau
Montpellier

29 May 1954

Dear Frieda,

Yesterday I received the catalogue of an English bookseller who specialises in modern books. Two items greatly interested me. Here they are:

115. A Large Collection of Unpublished Holograph Letters of NORMAN DOUGLAS. Some 70 letters, ca. 1933/50 to an intimate friend. Mainly personal letters, containing many frank remarks about well-known literary figures. There are a number of references to D. H. Lawrence. 'I read about D. H. Lawrence's grave but it didn't excite me. I can't get excited about Lawrence dead or alive. . . . But certainly his endless so-called admirers might have scraped up a pound or two.' He asks for details of the exhumation and for photographs; he is particularly interested in the skeleton.

Several pages later we have:

292 D. H. Lawrence. Last Poems, edited by Richard Aldington and Giuseppe Orioli. Orioli 1932. First edition (one of 750 copies). This copy presented to a friend of the author and publisher. It is inscribed by Frieda Lawrence, Norman Douglas, G. Orioli and Reginald Turner. A unique association copy. £7.10.0.

Can you remember to whom that copy was dedicated? I think it quite likely that this person was also the owner of the letters from Norman.

You can see how treacherous Norman was by that one remark quoted from those letters. He really hated Lorenzo, and I wonder why we were such duffers to be so slow in finding it out.

The mystery about Pino's books deepens. A writer in the Times Lit Supp about two years back (Willy King, I think) stated definitely that Norman told him he re-wrote the books entirely. Now comes another 'friend', asserts he saw the MSS, and that Norman only made corrections! They must have been pretty extensive to include so many of his favourite clichés and writing tricks; or Pino must have had as great a gift for imitating Norman's literary style as Lorenzo had for making fun of people. But it doesn't matter whether Pino's hand or Norman's hand wrote the script. The essential is that in 1930–32 Pino was enthusiastic for L., and under Norman's nagging turned against him and published those lies I have tried to expose. What Norman's friends are printing now is that I wrote Pinorman to revenge myself because Pino left me out of Moving Along! Now you must have seen the reason both for publishing that letter in facsimile in which Pino expresses gratitude for the 100 pounds he never repaid, and for exposing the silly little lies about our motor trip. If he were ungrateful to me, why not to you and Lorenzo? If he published lies about me, why not about Lorenzo?

I don't know whether your letter has been printed or not. Frere certainly said he had sent it in, but since then he has not mentioned it. I expect there has been a conference of Monty Mackenzie, Nancy [Cunard], etc., over it, to decide whether it shall be published with abuse and sneers of you, or whether some excuse shall be found to refuse it. The English papers which have published this abuse of me absolutely refuse to print any reply from me, however mild! Aren't they wonderful? As Dr Johnson said: 'Are we still alive after all this ~~abuse~~ satire?'

I still have not got the exact date for Lawrence of Arabia, but I am promised all the contracts by 4th June. Well, I've been promised them before and haven't received them. But this time I've written very peremptory directions, and hope I may succeed. The contracts should have been prepared long ago, and not left to the last minute like this. It is really maddening.

Did I tell you that Houghton Mifflin have asked to see Pinorman with a view to an American edition? I don't think they'll take it—not the sort of thing to go in Boston! But Professor [Mark] Schorer mentioned a small firm he knows in N.Y. [Grove Press] who are trying to do Lady C.; and they might take it. There is no use going to the usual crowd; they wouldn't touch it. There has been great difficulty in finding a publisher for the Lawrence of Arabia book, but we've got one at ~~one~~ last. If only those blasted lawyers would stop dawdling over the contracts! I really could pistol them.

The row about Pinorman is as nothing to the row there will be about Lawrence of Arabia—a lot of very eminent people are exposed. What worries me so about these continuous delays is that I know they, including Churchill, are moving Heaven and Earth to persuade the publishers not to issue the book, while they circulate lies about me in the newspapers. Once the contracts are signed, I am tranquil. Until that, I may still be betrayed.

How do you like this? Just to make sure, some kind person sent an underlined copy of Monty Mackenzie's article to Catherine!

All love to you both,
Richard

13 June 1954

Dear Richard,

Angie liked your story of the great feast and said in Europe these feasts will always exist, come hell or high water. 'Richard could never live in England again', he told one.

I am glad your Catha has such a good time. Send me a photograph of her, will you?

Frere sent me another 'Time and Tide' and this is my answer, it scares me a little, there are so many flourishing pansies around. I told Frere to send it or not as he thinks best. With this I come out in the open and they may say I invented it. It's God's truth—

Love to you
Frieda

No wonder that in England the horses are more important than the individuals! It must have been a splendid feast!

To Time and Tide—

It does not much matter what Miss [Nancy] Cunard says to glorify Douglas at L's expense. The world has taken the measure of L more or less especially the young. I dont think Miss C doesn't seem very bright, not profoundly so.

I did not want to tell this story, it is an ugly one, but now I will.

When I was in Florence after L was dead, to talk with Orioli about his publishing some of L's books, I was in Orioli's flat and Norman was there too. Casually Norman said to me: I have got a charming boy of 14 but I prefer them younger, wouldn't you like to take him on?' He would never have said that to me while L. was alive. I said after gathering my wits: 'I have children of my own.'

I don't know whether Miss C thinks I would have felt honored by kind Douglas' offer or not. I was horrified and never saw him again.

I have a photograph of Miss Cunard that Orioli and Douglas sent me. She wears a bathingcap like a helmet and looks very striking and handsome.

El Prado
Taos
New Mexico

[c. 15 June 1954]

Dear Richard,

You have your hands full or rather your fists ready for the fray! The mealy-mouthed ones! (An L. word) that Nancy C!

[Nancy Cunard] I know the little Lord Fauntleroy that Norman could put on. I should not think profound understanding was her (N.C.'s) strong point! The book Pinorman has come, it looks nice, the photograph of the bust of Norman, very good. I had some good ones, young ones of Pino, but I was so angry when his book came, that I tore them up—The point of Pinorman is that it is a unique thing, recreating a unique relationships between a few people; apart from moral issues. In the future it will be appreciated! But anything but the truth! Put the whitewash on, lots of it!

Pino's book came in italian too! Angie says Mondadori would like to print 'Pinorman'.

Frere loves you, you are lucky, he has a genius for friendship. I know about the 'formula' writing from young writers, why don't the publishers write the books? They do practically!

In Houston L is a communist. In Austin they want to make a centre of L study on a big scale for all America, even the world, so it goes! I must get your Lawrence of Arabia book. Surely they can't sue you for libel, it's all true in Pinorman! In fact you left out the worst things about him, I know the stories about the wife!

I was thinking how truly kind you were to L in Port-Cros, when he wasn't well and cross and we were having such fun, you as a bullfighter with that donkey! Did you never write about Napoleon? You know so much and what's more you made me understand the quality of his mystic power over men.

You know about genius! You have even given Norman his due and his glamour of wickedness, one is never sorry for him, you never make him 'small beer' nor Pino either! Norman even might have appreciated the picture of himself! Don't get involved with them on moral issues, you don't get anywhere with them that way, insist on the human, actual presentation of men as you found them.

That Catha of yours will go a long way, I can see that!

Frere can take it, I am sure!

So all good luck and love to you both from me and Angie too, he is most interested!

If you see the man [F.-J.] Temple will you tell him I will write soon, please, we are so busy doing all the Mss and so on! Angie <u>loves</u> Pinorman!

15 July 1954

Dear Richard,

I would have written before, but I wanted to copy the maltese letter for you, and I have hunted for it and can't find it again. We put the Mss and other stuff in order, there is so much, I must look some more. It is a long letter.

I loved the Roy letter. That's how to get at them. He has courage that man! So the 'Lawrence of Arabia' will come out, you certainly never seem to have a dull moment. I shall be very interested to read it.—My, but they will squeal again! What is C.B.E.? Do you mean he will be a Lord, Frere? What fun! He is terribly clever. He is really a rebel at heart, yet he manages 'them' so cleverly, that they don't know it.

I finally wrote to Mr. Temple. O, and I have not thanked you yet for the charming photographs of Catha! I like her soft face, not like an american hardboiled one! She looks so alive! Your part of the world sounds rather wonderful, I find bits written about it in odd places! The world is moving so fast, it rushes along. That McCarthy [witch-hunting] business was strange to listen to, a bit like Cicero and Caesar and Pompey, only on a lower plane.

I get an awful lot of visitors. I avoid them as much as I can.—I always loved your 'Spirit of Place'.

There might be lots more I have wanted to say, but I better send this now—I am very flourishing financially, you will be glad to hear. It's good in one's old age, but sorry Lorenzo could never be lavish, he might have enjoyed it, but I know he would not have begrudged it one!

Yours ever,
Frieda

Angelino sends greetings, he is a great help—

El Prado

29 August 1954

Dear Richard,

I haven't written because you can't imagine what propor-
tions L's work seems to have taken on! More than I can digest!

First this may interest you, the university of Texas is making
a big Lawrence centre and wants to buy all the stuff we will let
them have and I know they would buy all your letters and I
don't know what else, you might have. They are very rich, oil
lands! They even want to buy the ranch (I would give them the
small hill and the chapel) to make a sort of place for students
to work there. We are both pleased with this, as it solves the
problems of the ranch. I hope you like the idea. They are very
keen. Your own books they will want too. Now you write, if
you wish of course, to Prof. Warren Roberts, 3015 West
Avenue, Austin, Texas. This young man came to talk things
over. And the dean writes clear and keen letters.—

Now about the Norman thing. After getting rid of my
indignation, I feel milder about him. In one way he had a fine
idea of hospitality. He was not small beer. There was one side
that <u>was</u> superior and individual. Can you understand this,
that I feel like that? There is so much small stuff around—I
don't go back for one moment ~~of~~ on what I said, but I think
you are perhaps more effective if you give the devil his
due.—Yes, quote my letters, quote this bit too, if you like. So
many people, o dear! Wonderful weather, with a bit of
autumn in it!

Love to you both—
Frieda

I like your address!

El Prado

24 September 1954

Dear Richard,

What you wrote about Frere distressed me very much. Do
tell me all about it. I wanted to write to him, then I thought I
might only be a nuisance.—I always knew at some time he
would clash with the stuffed shirts and dumb ones and too

smart ones! He is a rebel at heart. He also has a real gift for friendship, I mean male friendship without the 'trimmings' so rare nowadays. I realized long ago what a friend he was to you. You could not have a better one.

We are terrible busy, about copyrights and 'Sons and Lovers' as a movie and a man, Jake Zeitlin is coming from Los Angeles to appraise the Mss and so on, that are left.

You have no idea what a mess Lawrence's work is in America! Frere is printing an awful lot of L's books! You see in England all is in the hands of Pollinger and Frere! Pollinger has been a very good agent to me, I don't have to bother but I bother about America, but it's no use, they are too smart for me! Well, I won't go nuts over it!

The University of Texas sounds really keen and decent people. Texas is keen on 'Culture', but I hear they want it easy, spoonfed! They might like your own Mss.—All that has to do with L.—Fortunately Angelino is quite interested in making those dull lists and things with a secretary, I don't.

Willie Maugham would be good, I am sure about Pinorman and would be with you there. Is he still quite energetic? Do you think Frere will lose? How hopeful it is!

We have had weeks of heavenly weather!

All good things to you and Catherine!

Greetings from Angie

Ever the old
Frieda

Box 201
Port Isabel
Texas

5 December 1954

Dear Richard,

Your clippings about T. E. Lawrence came to-day, just as I had been longing to have a talk with you. My sister Else had sent me a publisher called Lisk's book. There was a bit by T.E.L. and Winston Churchill on him, as he sees him, as a superman. T.E.L. describes an arab feast. Not convincing. He does not say how that awful mess they ate, all terribly greasy, was cooked on what kind of a fire, it might be Baedeker!

What was the man after? One could have sympathy with lots of people. The Albanians, Americans and England had before helped the Jews in Palestine. He must have had some hypnotic quality. It will be terribly interesting to read your book. But you have let off an atomic bomb! How did you find out? He must have hypnotised <u>himself</u>. Of course Churchill is a swashbuckler himself. It must have been fun for you to discover that man under all his masquerade. But I shudder when I think how they will go for you, taking their 'seven pillars' away from them! Seven pillars of swindle! I do hope I hear soon that Frere has won his case! The law is still the same as in 1868! I am happy to be here, Padre Island with its still wild sea and a long beach, and pelicans, gulls big and enormous and small and cranes and ducks and wild geese—and lovebirds that fly over from Mexico and come around! It is spring-like and I can swim, not very far, there are little, ugly sharks. Very few people and I have <u>time</u>, time to be myself!

They gave us a great reception at Austin, glad that's over! I am so excited about this Lawrence business! I have often been asked if I had been <u>his</u> wife! <u>wife</u> indeed! This is just in a hurry!

My best wishes for you and your lovely child and a merry Xmas! Angie is trying to understand the income tax! No income tax in the Lawrence days! He sends his best wishes.

—Frieda

It must be fun going shopping in Montpellier.

Box 201
Port Isabel
Texas

14 February 1955

Dear Richard,

That Rumpusdragon is truly 'formidable'! My, oh my is it possible that you really put salt on their tails? I thought they were so secretly and secretly entrenched! Three cheers for you! 'Prince of Mecca' are they really so childish! You have really done something, cleared the air and caned them! It gives one hope! Angie was pleased too. It took a lot of courage.

I hope it does some good in America too, America needs it so badly!

I am very sad to-night. Had a letter from Grace Hubble, widow of Edwin Hubble, the Palomar scientist, that they have given up all hope of Maria Huxley.—I have not heard anymore. She has always been a loyal friend, when the Ottoline–Bertie crowd were so bad to me. Poor Aldous; she was a good wife, read to him by the hour. But she was always frail.—

Thank you for the postcards you sent, and the french article with the charming photograph of father and daughter!

And that you are getting rich is also not to be sneezed at!

Angelino says he prefers rich friends, then you don't have to bother about them! Now I close, just to say how I share the excitement—

But I am sad about Maria! I was very fond of her—

Love
Frieda

I should have written you on some swanky paper I got for Xmas, but I find it easier writing on lines! I am looking forward to the book!

Les Rosiers
Ancien chemin de Castelnau
Montpellier

19 February 1955

Dear Frieda,

I am sorry to hear this news of Maria Huxley. It is almost a death sentence to Aldous too, for who now will look after him? He will have to shave his head, buy a yellow robe, a razor and a rice bowl, and become a Buddhist saint like [Earl] Brewster. How Lorenzo would have jeered at Brewster for going into a monastery!

By the way, why was Aldous so high and mighty that he wouldn't record memories of Lorenzo for that BBC man? It is true most of Lorenzo's friends were poor and humble people, but Lady Cynthia did not disdain to take part. I don't get it. True, we want people to read L's books instead of gossiping about him; but it is natural to want to preserve the memories of the few who knew him.

Did you know Frere and [Pat Wallace, Mrs Frere] Wallace were in New York, and have now gone by plane to N. Zealand and Australia? Frere wanted a change after all that business of his, and I suspect also wanted to be out of England for my Rumpus. He was very scared because it was through him I collected old Churchill's testimony, by a question which showed that TEL was a liar. Later, Churchill tried to shuffle out of it! But I don't wonder Frere was troubled. He had to stand eight times in the Old Bailey dock, and all for a piece of malice on the part of a newspaper owner who acted as common informer via the press. Frere wanted to sue him after the 'not guilty' verdict, but to his fury the lawyers said he couldn't! Yet he still goes on saying, if not thinking, that England is the most wonderful country, 'salt of the earth' etc. But he has always been a most wonderful friend to me, and still is. I was most touched that he paid to have all the reviews of my TEL book sent by air to N.Y., and though they are raving against me, he sent me the message: 'You've won!' when he heard that Collins had ordered a third impression making at least 40,000 copies in the first week.

Did I tell you Christina Foyle sent me a letter of congratulation, adding that their shop is 'selling so many copies'? I am told they have a whole window display with the huge scroll: 'Is This The End Of A Legend?' Collins were very clever. They found out that TEL's friends had got hold of all the 'upper class' newspapers and weeklies, and intended to try and kill the book. Collins had taken at least 1,000 pounds' worth of advertising space. They cancelled the lot, and spent the money on having window displays all over London and England! The booksellers were very pleased, of course, and tell their customers what a fine book it is. And the 'enemies' made such huge headlines that they did the newspaper advertising! Of course they took in a lot of suckers, but most people said, 'What is there in this book that they're making such a fuss about?'

Collins also spent about £1,500 on lawyers' fees to get the evidence legally 'vetted' and to secure further evidence where it was legally needed. I think it is one up to me that they eventually found this evidence though nobody knew it existed. Wasn't it funny that Jix [Sir William Joynson-Hicks, Lord Brentford] was my lawyer, after the old man persecuted Lorenzo and I had insulted all I could? They were very anti-me at first, but when together we found that legal proof of the bastardy they changed round and became enthusiastic. My warmest fan letters come from detectives, barristers and senior officers. Full Generals and Air Marshals and Peers are now wrangling about TEL in the D. Telegraph! And they of course are advertising the book without realising it!

There is going to be a display on Radio France on the 7th March. A great enthusiast here is Detective-Inspecteur Delarue, one of their most brilliant younger men, who also writes a little. He looks at the book professionally, as a very careful piece of detection! Well, after some trouble (because Radio France have twice reviewed the book) Delarue and my friend Kershaw were allowed 5 minutes for their weekly 45 mins programme. But you are allowed to talk up to 15 minutes, which is recorded and they select what they want. Well, Delarue got interested and went extempore his full 15 mins. When he and Alister came out of the recording room, they were met by two directors, a producer and two editors who had been listening. The whole 15 minutes will be used without a word cut, they will read extracts from the book, I am to say my little piece, and in short the whole 45 mins on the 7th March goes to that book. In addition a weekly called Noir et Blanc will run a double-page spread by Delarue, while Le Miroir de l'Histoire is going to interview Alister and get from him the story of how TEL's friends (including Sir W.!) tried in an underhand way to get the book suppressed. Alister was my agent, and has ALL the letters involved. So if he does that job right, there will be another pleasant surprise for those O so honest Britanniques.

Since publication day I have written three articles for London papers—Illustrated (100 pounds), Daily Sketch (£40) and Daily Mail (£25).

The anti-fan letters would amuse you both, they are so like the Lady C. letters. 'You ought to be horse-whipped and sent to Liberia' says one. Another says he is not going to read my book because I have smeared a great hero and he knows the book is bad. Another one—an obvious fairy—sends me digestive tablets. But the officers of the Old Army are enthusiastic, and

I have strings of generals and staff colonels sending me praise and also more evidence against him. One of the most important who wrote to the Telegraph is General Sir George de S. Barrow, G.C.M., K.C.M.G., who commanded the 4th Cavalry Division of Allenby's army, saw TEL in the battle! and formed a very low opinion of him. Now, so arrogant and stupid are TEL's friends, that one of them named [Liddell] Hart wrote to the D.T. [*Daily Telegraph*] practically calling General Barrow a liar—and Barrow is the most senior living officer of the old Indian Army!

Such fun! Wish you were near enough to share. The book was sent to El Prado for you.

Love to both from us both,
Richard

Box 201
Port Isabel
Texas

8 March 1955

My dear Richard,

Last night came your T.E.L. and I read it on and off all night, I read and went to sleep and woke up again and read some more and it made a profound impression on me as a whole—The background too. What a man, not a scrap of feeling, not anywhere! not at any moment of his life! What an indictment of politics and loathsome propaganda and greed and lies, what a gigantic mess! It gives one shudders! I think you did a great service and a courageous one to your fellowcountrymen and all the rest of the world! It is unforgettable! Lawrence would have loved it, I mean one can't love it but what you did with it! And you are fair! No spite and you give the devil his due! But it is so convincing, 'they' can't get around it! 'Love for the Arabs', as L's father said, you remember when you talked to me at Port-Cros about Napoleon, I knew then that you had that special gift of unravelling and stating what goes on in the inside of people.—

I have had a great loss: Maria Huxley died. She was a loyal friend always. When the Ottoline crowd were so nasty to me, she was not. We never had a nasty word, she never hurt me.

Had a lovely letter from Aldous, her death did something to
him. He helped her to die with love and compassion. He will
miss her so very much—Died of cancer, 55. He will visit us in
Taos in the spring.
   How hard you must have worked! No wonder the French
like the book and the british army will too! The trouble is
people are helpless against that kind of impudence.—He
looks a melancholy bird in his photographs! I hate the
Freudian explanations, impudence is impudence! Angie flew
to Buenos Aires to visit his sister, I have my german Ida with
me, my children's old nurse and we rattle away in german. She
tells me much about Germany. We are lucky to have a nice
man to drive us when we want him. It is warm and green and
Padre Island is still wild and good.—
   The Americans must have your book. I don't wonder it sells
like hot cross buns!
   I had to say something quickly!

Yours ever,
Frieda

I never said 'thank you' but I feel thank you!

Box 201
Port Isabel
Texas

14 March 1955

My dear Richard,
   Now, don't get discouraged, but it makes me mad too!
Because strangely enough you have created, I say really
created, a living person that is interesting and convincing. I
think part of their rage is a compliment to you for your good
job; It is a work of art and will live, I got very interested in that
Lawrence, him in his inventiveness in building himself up as a
hero with the help of others. I believe there are many like
him.—The soldiers know, those that saw him at work—And
let the fate of Lady C console you, if yours had been a dead and
dull book, they would have ignored it. Those 'mills of God'
you know, give them time. And the mess you reveal (that's
wrong) is such an accusation. When that old swashbuckler has

joined other swashbucklers of the past, it will be different.—
That Lawrence was such a mischief maker, it is astounding!
Not a scrap of goodwill anywhere!—Yes, my sister Else wrote
to me from Heidelberg 'the young men, we know don't want
militarism in any form whatsoever'. They have it forced on
them! That's amusing about the taxes! Here the taxes are also
an awful <u>pest</u> and they put you in prison if you make mistakes.
You know I have my children's old german nurse with me, she
is a clever woman and she tells me about things; it seems so
american in Germany and though they aren't so poor
anymore, somehow I don't like the smell of it—Everybody is
afraid of his own shadow till they become shadows.—Angie is
in Buenos Aires, he visits his sister who is blissfully happy, he
means Italy and home to her. They are making a film of 'Sons
and Lovers' in Hollywood, I take the money and hope for the
best. Yes, Poor Aldous!—
  I shall be glad to see your Australian friends! How I would
love to eat a good bouillabaisse again! That book must come
out in America! Has that Lowell Thomas so much influence?
  Cheer up, the spring will do the trick!
  It's an uneasy world, an 'ill sitting hen'!

Yours ever,
Frieda

Les Rosiers
Montpellier

18 March 1955

My dear Frieda,
  I got some news yesterday. The German version of my TEL
book is being made by Ursula von Hohenlohe. Do you know
her? She must surely be a grande dame? My agent says she is
considered the best translator of English in modern Germany,
hopes to finish by May, and the publisher will come out with it
in the late summer. It will be nice to have a good German
version, as the French one is so bad. They made silly cuts (out
of avarice) and all sorts of little blunders and gave it a wrong
title. However, it seems to sell.
  The complications of this idiotic 'modern' world are past
belief—and above all they create infinite difficulties for an

author. I asked the Jap publisher to send you a copy of the Jap version of my Lorenzo book. Did you get it? I found that though the Americans allow journalists to draw and even American authors, it is hopeless for an English author. So I gave the 100,000 yen to a Japanese student. Getting money from Italy or Germany is a long misery. I have to wait months and months for Mondadori's royalties. And this German translation had to be done through a German agent in Switzerland, who is able to transfer money from W. Germany to Suisse, and then has a 'strong currency' which goes anywhere. I still have to get Bank of England permission for every pound coming from England, and they deduct 45% income tax on every pound. It is simply vindictive, and the Americans, who began it all, are just as bad. They want to crush any independent writers, and use these tax laws to do it. The German publisher of my Heldentod is the List Verlag of Leipzig, and I haven't heard from them for years. I suppose the book is out of print, though I was told by a Swedish journalist that he had seen copies circa 1949 in East Berlin.

I keep meaning to ask you if Lorenzo ever read Mistral, and if so what he thought? I can't find any mention of Mistral in the books. Very likely the outwardly classical form and long narrative poems would have put L. off; the Mistral's memoirs of his early [sic] make a charming book and all his prose is fun. Moreover there are lots of passages in the poems which L. would have liked. Mistral really had an ambience of his own, lived with and inspired the people of Provence, persuaded the women to wear the lovely old costumes, kept the dances and songs and festivals going. It was very much what L. wanted to do, and couldn't because the people didn't exist for him. No poet in modern times has had such a following among the people as Mistral and that without the slightest bit of playing down or vulgarity of any kind. His influence still lasts, though of course the damned Paris govt., the great alcohol trusts and the industrialists are rapidly destroying it. I am trying to do a little book on Mistral, though I know those London fairies will sneer at it as 'folk-lore'—as if folk-lore were not a million times better that their 'Dummheit-lore'. If L. had ever got really interested in Mistral how wonderfully he would have written about it all.

They haven't changed in London at all about L. There are

two fellows . . . writing a book on the Café Royal. They asked me about my memories, which are very few indeed. Here is what one of them says: 'Your lucid and impartial book on DHL almost made me accept the pre-supposed "genius", but JMM and the hagiographers will insist on their "prophet"! I find it very hard to read that folkloristic staccato, and his passages of oh so benign introspection, forever addressing himself to a cénacle of sandal-shod elderly apostolettes who couldn't wait to carry slops for him in the next Rananim [Lawrence's ideal colony]. Were these constant arrangements for his forthcoming crucifixion really necessary to make him write nearly as well as Arnold Bennett?'

There you are, you see. Plus ça change. . . . And there you have them making those same old foolish wise-cracks against a real writer and man, and going into transports of rage at my exposure of their phoney Colonel 'Lawrence'. The personal bitterness against me is really astounding—it is just the same sort of abuse as those Lady C. reviews, and just as unfair.

There was a very nice two-page illustrated article about the book and me in Wednesday's 'VUE', which has a very large circulation in France. The amusing thing is that the Lycéennes of course read it, and yesterday one of the editors of their journal (*Vol d'Essai*) came with Catha to interview me. I made most of it fun, of course, and ended up with a story of how the Colonel pretended he had hung his Croix de Guerre on the neck of a dog in Oxford, which always fetches the French—an insult to La Patrie! Then the two girls in high excitement flew off to the local paper and selected one of their unpublished photos of me, and later attended the council of profs who decide what can go in. Apparently, with some slight changes their contribution was accepted. I only hope C. won't want to be a writer.

I was thinking this morning that it is just 25 years since L. died, and that if he had lived he would still be only 70. Strange to think of.

Our love to you and Angie,
Richard

Les Rosiers
Ancien chemin de Castelnau
Montpellier

21 March 1955

My dear Frieda,
   You give so much strength and courage in your letters—I
see more and more how you helped Lorenzo in all that fierce
battle. I wish I could believe that this book of mine had a
hundredth part of the value of Lady C. It hasn't. It is only
'documentation' but they hate it because it is the truth, and
they love only lies and the liars.
   I am so happy to hear that 'Sons and Lovers' is to be filmed,
and hope you have been well paid. Of course nothing of the
'genius' will or could get into Hollywood, but it doesn't matter.
The book is always there. The Americans are so stupid, they
know nothing, feel nothing. But a German or Russian cinéaste
might make a masterpiece of Sons and Lovers. It could be
done. Hollywood is all lies. The other day I saw a Charlie
Chaplin film, supposed to be so wonderful—the one satirising
industrialism and the 'depression'—and it is moronic, with all
those yahoo American wasting-food 'jokes'. And the slick
communistic propaganda. I hated it.
   On top of the news that my German edition is secure, I had
an air-mail from my N.Y.Bank to-day showing that the South
American edition is secure and the advance paid. The battle
for the USA edition goes on, but I have hopes, now that these
two are secured. When I get America we have the main areas
and languages— English, Spanish, German and French. The
Italians hang fire, though Mondadori himself (the good
Alberto whom I like so much because he resembles Pino a
little) wrote me he wanted the book. And then got frightened
by the reviews. Ach. Why are they all such cowards?
   Did I tell you about Alberto Mondadori in Paris in 1946? He
was then about 28, married, of course, with two children he
adored, but terrified of his father who made the business such
a great success. To get this story you must remember that the
Mondadori are millionaires in dollars. Well, Alberto got to see
me in Paris, because his father wanted to link up with their old
authors. (By the way, Italy alone paid me the royalties earned
by my books during the war—in England there was no paper
for anything but war propaganda!) The meeting was a little

formal, but we soon began to thaw, and I must have said something to encourage Alberto. He looked at me, laughing, and said—so like Pino—'Isn't it funny, only two years ago I was wearing a black shirt!' I roared with laughter, shook hands, ordered a bottle of champagne, and all went well. Then he told me a real Pino story about himself. In the Rue de Seine he had found a wonderful relic of la belle époque—an imitation telephone box of 1900. You stood in front of it and said sharply: 'Deux verres!' and it flew open and presented two glasses and a bottle of vermouth or something. 'It would please my friends in Milano so much, they would be happy' he said. 'Why didn't you buy it?' 'Ma ché. It costs 40,000 francs'. (In those days $400 and heaven knows how much in lire!) Knowing how rich the family is I said, 'Well, it's an absurd price, but as you want it so much . . .?' 'My father!' he said, looking like a frightened little boy, 'How could I justify it to my father?' Of course I should have bought it for him. But can't you see those wealthy Milanese saying 'Deux verres!' to the telephone box with inexhaustible delight?

I am glad you have the old Nurse with you. She is right about the Americanisation. They have just stepped in and tried to dominate, exploit and remould the world. They are just as vile as the Russians and Brits. Worse because so powerful. They hate the French because the French don't respond—just take no notice. I admire them so much for it. You know that Coca-Cola is a sign of American supremacy, advertised on old Italian buildings and even on the Grand Canal in Venice. Well, to their rage, Pétain put through laws, still valid, which forbid bill-posting on buildings and even along the roads. (Italy is quite ruined by the ads. and not one exists in France.) But they may advertise in Cafés and even, within severe limits, on the outside of Cafés. I was at the Saintes Maries on a hot day while Catha was riding, and seeing the Coca-Cola ads, remembered a friend had told me that iced C-C with a dash of rum is the best hot weather drink. I ordered it. 'We've plenty of rum, but no Cola-Cola', said the garçon. 'Pourtant,' I said 'You have all these ads.' 'Yes, but no one here ever drinks that stuff—we put up the ads to please the Americans. Un bock bien froid? Bon.' Don't you love it?

Yes Lowell Thomas has the most influential TV programme in the East, and CBS is entirely on his side, as well as much of the press. But I begin to think we may get it through. Over the week-end the abuse of me in the English press was simply incredible, because I think they realise they are losing. Not only are the fan letters all on my side now, but I hear that the sales are picking up again. They were almost killed for a time. But people are reading and recommending the book. I have a letter from a parson in Staffordshire (Lorenzo's 'own Midlands') apologising for having doubted me, and saying that the writer is now convinced that T. E. Lawrence was 'three parts a charlatan'.

Now they want me to do d'Annunzio. And I think he really was a great man. But it will mean so much work, and I wonder if I can get access to the Italian archives? If the communists ~~may~~ have destroyed the evidence? But after destroying a phoney English hero, what fun to make a real Italian one! Will you ask Angie what he thinks about it?

You could make bouillabaisse at Port Isabel. The saffron has to be ordered from a drug store, but they can get it. You need a very fierce fire, about a tumbler of olive oil, ditto of white wine, water, potatoes peeled and quartered, lots of garlic, a tomato, rosemary, fennel, laurel, thyme, and at least one lobster with the fish. If you make a fish soup of crabs and fish instead of water, it is delicious. You can make it—only remember very hot fire to make the oil absorb!

Love to you both,
Richard

Les Rosiers
Ancien chemin de Castelnau
Montpellier

1 April 1955

My dear Frieda,
I love your suggestion about 'hagiographers' being old hags—they were mostly fat-headed old men anyway, Calabrian monks and so forth. It is one of those compound Greek-derived words—'hagios', holy, saint and 'grapho' write, i.e. writings about saints or writers about saints, and more balderdash to the square inch than in most books.

Geoff Dutton, the Australian ex-airman who sent those

photographs of the Mirenda—they are good, don't you think?—has just sent me a letter in English written by Grato Mariani, a Florentine, who says of Pinorman: 'When writing to Aldington do please tell him that the substance of his book is very much alive for me, even if I was only a boy then (strangely enough Reggie Turner's face is the one I remember best of the group) and that the young ones (so to speak) like me, do most certainly not feel unconnected with it all. But perhaps it is because he tells of Florence, or because I feel he was happy to re-live the company, the vino, the atmosphere of those days, and thus has made me happy also about them: non so. I'd like him to know anyway, and know that as a florentine I thank him for the resurrection of Orioli to immortality (an adopted florentine, but a true convert to il Cupolone).'

This is the first decent thing which has been said about Pinorman apart from those two noble letters you wrote. I just saw Mariani in Firenze at Xmas—he looked nice, but belonged to one of those Viale familes, you know? Anyway, perhaps someday even Pinorman will come out of the lies, and that vindication of Lorenzo be accepted. Strangely enough, I believe you and I are the only ones who know how mean Norman was in making Pino write that anti-Lorenzo stuff. And, don't believe Pino wasn't mean about you, he was. Unfortunately, this happened—Pino sent me a Lorenzo picture with a letter in which he said nasty things about you. When I left Brigit, she stole it and it has now been sold in America with Pino's letter abusing you for meanness to me! He, instigated by Norman, was trying to put me against you. I ought to have destroyed the letter, but I kept it in order to refute it—and then Brigit stole and sold picture and letter! What next?

Thank you very much for telling me about the airman, and his report on the newspapers. I now understand why the BBC is sending out propaganda to America against me and the book.

The battle goes on, in England, and they are trying to draw me into it by making outrageous insults. I am being wonderfully defended by a splendid man called Rob Lyle, a great friend of Roy Campbell, known in the British Leftist press as 'the Fascist beast'! He is truly noble in his generosity, and they hate him because he is such a brilliant polemical (from Gk 'polemos' a fight!) writer. He has reduced one of the worst 'TEL' defenders to silence, and is now tackling the really most vicious. Did I tell you that we now call 'Colonel' T E Lawrence 'the Moocher'? Roy Campbell (a great poet) has written a Preface to Geoffrey Dutton's book on Africa, Roy being a South African. In the course of it he mentions how he, the Duttons, Kershaw and I at Villa Aucassin discussed L. when I began the book thinking L. a hero; and Roy warned me he knew from General Nogales (commander of the Turkish cavalry) that he wasn't. Roy goes on: 'He (i.e. TEL) owed more of the spurious admiration he enjoyed to mooching about in a gyppo's nightie in the London suburbs than to soldiership on the battlefield.' ('Gyppo' is English soldier slang for 'Egyptian'!) Isn't that fun?

I'm fighting back. I have just sent a letter to Randolph Churchill (I was told in 1915 not to trouble the Great Man any more!) in which I very politely show that Winston has signed a lie to defend his phoney friend! I don't know how they can get out of it.

Have you heard that Eastwood is to build a memorial to Lorenzo 'an immense social and cultural centre'! I've only just heard from a friend in the Midlands, and I laughed. The silly fools who exiled him, who insisted his pictures were taken out of England, who haven't got his MSS! Don't let them have a scrap if they ask you. Just send them this quotation slightly altered from Johnson to Chesterfield:

'Is not a patron one who looks with unconcern on a man struggling for life in the water, and, when he has reached ground, encumbers him with help? The notice you have been pleased to take of my late husband's labours, had it been early, had been kind; but it has been delayed until he has been long dead; until I am solitary and cannot share it, until he is known and it is not needed.' Give it to them, Frieda. Do you know that one of the lies they keep printing about me is that I have written <u>depreciating</u> Lorenzo! Is there anyone who has worked harder and longer for him? Until I published that Portrait of a Genius But . . . the full story had never been told in England and it stopped much of the calumny. And now the same papers which praised that book are printing that I am an enemy of Lawrence who 'denigrated' him! I suppose every Churchill gets the country he deserves.

Do try to see the Duttons when they cross USA. They are very nice—not London, you know, but warm-hearted and Australian. I think she is very pretty....

Yes, those Café Royal pansies. Of course I didn't answer [their letter], but that type of fairy seems all-powerful in England now. I was staggered the other day to hear that Churchill favours them! Certainly, we know what Eddie Marsh was. And then there was Kitchener and his 'young men'. And then C. and his fulsome praises of the 'Moocher'. Horrid, isn't it? They are trying hard to get rid of him, I'm told, but the old Beefeater won't go.

Love to you both from me and Catha,
Richard

[c. April 1955]

Dear Richard,

Another gay letter from you to-day! Hurrah! Angie came home and I had to read your letters to him and he loved the stories about Mondadori and the Coca Cola waiter. He says why not ask Mondadori to help you with the D'Annunzio. I don't know why there is such a difference between the genuine 'show-off' of a D'Annunzio and the shoddy one of a Col. L—I lent the book to the handsome young flier and he was very much impressed. He said: 'but he is convincing'. The truth seems to have a good smell of its own, that propaganda never has, can't have. I was so shocked reading a german paper 'der Mondt'. You know 'Darkness at Noon' by Arthur Köstler which I thought good. But in this last issue he writes about the 'Adventure in Spain'. Don't argue with them, just make a stench of them in the world. 'See to it that men curse them and shake themselves in horror', he was told.—This doesn't work in the long run. Your Col. L. is still a human being, if an unpleasant one, he still interests one.—It is awfully well written, it must have taken it out of you! How I loathe propaganda! The crime against the Holy Ghost!

Hardly anything has hurt me as much as when Pino, Pino who was so gentle with L, as patient as you were with L at

Port-Cros, ~~and~~ turned against him because of Norman and now you say he was nasty about me too! And Mondadori's story reminded me of Reggie Turner. Do you remember Pino found him practicing on his new phone: 'Yes, dear Lady Susan, I shall be delighted to come to lunch on Thursday and so on'—I am bad at those other root words, partly ignorance and partly I don't like them. You should have written that part of your discussion how you began your book when Roy called Col. L. a 'moocher' (what a lovely word for him) because I wondered how you got onto the Colonel's trail. But anyhow now it is written. 'A Gyppo nightie' it _is_ fun! Eastwood an immense social and cultural centre!! Have you _seen_ the place? Now they pat themselves on the back for having 'produced' Lawrence! What fun the gods must have! Can you believe it? _I_ being mean about you, when I had only had such fun at Port Cros, and admired your way with Lawrence and your gentleness with Brigit. Poor Pino, maybe he was already sick. Our lives would be much poorer without Pino. You must have been pleased to get that letter from Grado Mariani. Did you ever see something Pino had written on a tour with Norman in Austria about some boys they saw bathing in a mountain lake? The feeling was as it might be of some students seeing some young girls playing in the water—I just found an old letter from L, that made me think of you: He says something like this: 'Don't ask me for love, but back me in my fight, I have got to go about the world ~~to~~ fighting.' I thought how he would approve of you. There are a few, o so few real fighters!

It is already very hot—To-morrow I make the bouillabaisse! Angie enjoyed his glimpse of Mexico City and his flight over the Andes. He stayed with his sister, husband and children. She is still homesick for her village Fredozzio near Ravenna—I still have my german Ida with me, she keeps me so spick and span! And looks after me too much, I don't like being looked after! Love to you both. What is the child doing?

Angie, he is asleep upstairs in the heat, sends his best—

Yours ever,
Frieda—

Les Rosiers
Ancien chemin de Castelnau
Montpellier

13 April 1955

Dear Frieda,

Though you're a soldier's daughter, you're not a soldier, or you'd put your full address and exact date at the top of every letter. And never be one minute too soon or too late. Do you know a high-ranking British Naval Officer said to me that when the German Fleet was surrendered on the 11/11/18 a rendezvous was given in the North Sea by latitude and longitude at an exact minute. Each Fleet had several hundred miles to steam. Exactly, exactly to the minute each of the Grand Fleets arrived. And said this Officer: 'We knew before that our foes were worthy of us, but that was <u>chic!</u>'. . . .

The fact is that Churchillism has just ruined English intellectual life, with its crushing taxation and disdain for little 'scribblers'. He has almost literally stolen money subscribed for the BBC, cut the fees, and then charges 'income tax' of 45% on all copyright fees. I think the fee for my last Armistice Day 'soldier poem' was 7/6—a little over a dollar! Usually my royalties are weeks coming through the 'Exchange Control' and always docked 45%. BUT, I had articles about the 'Moocher' book in Daily Mail, Daily Sketch and Illustrated. The money came through in 3 days ~~days~~ without a penny deduction. You see, they're afraid of journalists, and hate poets.

What next!

There is a chance that a small monthly periodical will take up 'Pinorman' again. What nobody realises is that Norman, domineering over Pino, had left in those books a set of calumnies of Lorenzo which future historians would have accepted as fact. Only you and I knew the truth, because I don't think Aldous or Brett or Mabel did. So to save Lorenzo's honour I <u>had</u> to do that book—for which I have been vilified all over England and America. Why do they like dirty old buggers so much?

Talking of which—I wish you knew Roy Campbell who is wonderful. I had a long letter from him yesterday in which he complained very seriously that the London papers won't print

the letters he sends them defending me against the friends of
the Moocher. Now this is the sort of letter he sends:

'To the Editor of XYZ,
Sir,
      My great friend, General Nogales of the Turkish cavalry,
operating against that little bastard T. E. Lawrence, often told
me that 'Colonel' Lawrence had been buggered by practically
everything except the rhinos and female camels. I can't think
why you attack my friend Aldington who like me is a Soci of
the Provencal Félibrige and served in the same ranks. The
sight of T. E. Lawrence's fat feminine backside is a constant
annoyance to me, a senior N.C.O. who chased his bloody
Arabs hundreds of miles without being able to catch them,
though we had fast motor bikes . . .'

He is more fun than Pino, and a great poet. You MUST
read his 'Talking Bronco', and get his memoirs 'Light on a
Dark Horse'. You and Angie will love them. He is wonderful
and the most loyal and affectionate of friends. And his satires
on the London communist-fairies are beyond praise. They
tried to get him down, and he used to go and cuff their heads
for them, until they fled at the sight of him. He is a huge strong
South African! One night Auden or . . . or one of them
was giving a lecture against him. Roy, who is very lame from
his war wounds, came stamping in on his stick, and Auden was
so frightened he hid under the table! Roy cuffed him, made a
speech to the audience, and sent them away.
      After the war, though he had a bad wound and malaria, the
British War Office wouldn't pay him because he was South
African, and he had to work as a garçon plongeur in a
restaurant to feed his beautiful wife and daughters. Then
Desmond MacCarthy got him a job at the BBC—as a
producer, but Roy pretended he thought he was to be a
Commissionaire at the door:
      'So I put on me Sunday suit, man, and all me war medals,
and went down to see the bloke. I stood to attention and said
"Regimental-Sergeant-Major Campbell reporting for duty at
the door, Sir".' 'Oh, but Mr Campbell, you're to be one of our
producers!' 'I beg your pardon, Sir. I thought you wanted me

to touch my cap and open the taxi doors of your communist pansies like Auden and . . . !!'

He gets away with it. At some poetry reading a little twirp came up and tried to patronise him, saying he had written a 'good' review of Roy's poems. Whereupon Roy stood to attention and said: 'I thank you very much for those kind words, Sir. This is the proudest day of my life, Sir. And when I go home, Sir, I shall tell my wife and that will be the proudest day of her life too, Sir.'

My friend Alister witnessed that, and said the man was such a fool he didn't see the satire!

Love to both,
Richard

Box 201
Port Isabel
Texas

6 May 1955

Dear Richard,

It is nice of you to draw my attention to the carelessness which I believe is one of my worst faults!—So I will watch it! It is getting hot here and we are glad to go back on the 14th! My German Ida goes back too, on her freightboat to Germany. But the oleanders and lovely cactus and so many birds; a turtle just appeared near the front door! And not so many people. And the lovely gulf at Padre Island! Aldous came to see us. I was very fond of Maria! Theirs was an unusual and successful marriage. His outward world is shattered, she did so much for him, but in himself he is peaceful and has accepted his great loss. We talked a lot, he so naturally, also about Col. Lawrence—He was interested—from here he went to his son Matthew and his wife and 2 children.—He said: 'Maria made me more human', and her death made him more so, I think. They won't like you in England, you have taken their lollipops from them!! They don't like me either! I want to be charitable and think that Eastwood is doing this L memorial in a blind instinct, it is blind all right! You give a grim picture of english publishing! I do hope Frere is allright. I am very fond of Frere but I know he would be bouncy and I suppose it's like walking

on raw eggs, his publishing! I send you this article they asked
me to write, I think it will amuse you! Being 75 I get social
security. 98 dollars a month, good isn't it, just for being old!
Good bye for now, as Mabel says on the phone,

> Always yours—
> Frieda

> P.O. Box 201
> Port Isabel
> Texas

> 4 February 1956

Dear Richard,
  You sent me such a beautiful poem, I liked it very much, it
made me think of the England one loves. I hope you and the
child (that's how I think of her) are well and cheerful. We are
down here and have had warm lovely weather but it is raining
and not so warm at the moment, it has been very dry.—We
hear on the radio that Europe is very cold. I hope you can
keep warm.
  Your 'Lawrence of Arabia' book made a great impression I
think. We gave the upper ranch to the university of New
Mexico. I hope you like the idea. They are pleased to have it
and so are we to have this question settled. They want to build
cabins and have scholarships. I like to think of the place with
some worthwhile activity. What are you doing now, Richard?
We had quite a good income this year, but it's no use, the
income tax takes it nearly all. I wish they had a Poujade here!
We have television. It becomes a vice! We sit glued to it. Some
of it allright, some of it awful.
  When I see Coca-Cola I must think of your writing, how the
French don't like it. I also don't like the taste of it. Next week
we go to the stock-show in San Antonio, very texan!! We also
have friends there, they were our nice neighbours here,
General Pierce and his wife Kate. He has had to have an eye
out, what people go through—When we first knew them, he
was such a talker, now he lost his speech—We are both well
and peaceful—Those nice Australian people send me the
Bulletin, the paper Lawrence loved to read in Australia, you
know those friends you sent to Taos. L. only read 'Corriere
della Sera', before Mussolini and that Bulletin, of newspapers.

I ~~only~~ always thought the London Times was a 'stuffed shirt'.
But then there are so many stuffed shirts in England, so they
must have their paper. I wonder what you are writing about
now. Tell me, please! I heard from Julia, whom you may
remember, she was a young peasant girl who worked for us at
the Mirenda—How good they were! A man, Edward Nehls, is
writing a big book on L. He does not say anything himself,
only got the people who knew L. to have their opinion. Did he
write to you? It isn't quite fair, because L has no say. A bit
lopsided—How Douglas hated L! He told [Philip] Heseltine
nobody was sorry when L died! I have a stack of letters written
when L died, grieving over his death—That Elaine Luce is
trying to do something for Ezra Pound. That reminds me of
Mecklenburgh Square [1918 London residence] where he
appeared and we did not want him very much, none of
us.—Poor Ezra! How could anybody take those blackshirts to
their bosom!—He was not very bright! He paid for it and now
I think he has paid enough—

I am glad the spring is round the corner—there is the sun, I
am glad to say, how one misses it!

I hope this year will be a good one for you and the child! I
am peacefully reading Shakespeare; what monsters some of
his men are, so many of them, those Kings! And yet he gets
you!

Affectionately,
Frieda

I always like to write your fascinating address——

Les Rosiers
Ancien chemin de Castelnau
Montpellier

7 February 1956

Dear Frieda,

They are in such a mess still over here that letters from USA,
Canada, even Australia reach me sooner than those from
country England! Yesterday a letter from Henry Williamson
reached me—posted in N. Devon on the 31/1/56! But
the wonderful thing is that the real life goes on stronger than

ever, paying no attention to airplanes and Edens. I am glad you like Poujade. I am a Poujadiste. The movement will be crushed, for it is individualism against communists and bureaucrats and big business, which are crushing them (and us) out of existence with unfair and confiscatory taxation. I wrote an article on Poujade 6 months ago—nobody would publish it, and now that I am proved right I believe it is out in London. Too late.

I am very pleased you liked the poem, which was written in the early 1920s after Arabella and I moved from Hermitage to Aldermaston—which now has the first and largest nuclear fission factory in England! Commercial-industrial-machinism is a horrible new evil religion, persecuting the old beautiful world, as the beastly Xtians did in their time.

I am very glad you have given the old ranch to the University of N.M., and hope they will keep it and the Chapel for ever as a memorial. And I am glad that you and Angie found a place by the sea in Texas, for as we drove by I thought it was so beautiful, and longed for an extra life to live down there.

The cold has not been at all bad here, but they make a lamentation and give candles to the Virgin if it freezes. Of course that kills all their 'primeurs', so it is a good speculation to give La Sainte Vierge a 50-franc candle to keep off the frost. But this year she hasn't done it. They never punish her, but when other local saints (such as St Gent) don't send rain, they rush for his statue, beat him and throw him in a river, just to teach him! Then bring him back and give him some candles. I have tried to tell something of the life here in a little book on Mistral, the great poet, which Frere is reluctantly publishing and the Americans won't touch. Frere says it won't sell, and evidently thinks I was a fool to waste my time on someone who isn't known to the world of newspapers and TV. (One for you!) I haven't had the proofs yet, but I will send you a copy. [It was later published successfully by the Southern Illinois University Press.]

I am being persecuted for those books on Norman and the other sod-liar [T. E. Lawrence] just as Lorenzo was, without having his genius, which is rather unfair. The American reviews were worse than the English, if possible—I had dared to expose the lies of the great Lowell Thomas! After the abuse, now comes the boycott. A thing called The Peacock Press has just issued two lectures I gave at Columbia Univ. about 1939. Sims, the publisher, says he can scarcely sell any copies in England—more are bought in Japan! And the BBC returned the book with contempt, saying they would neither review it, nor use any of it for broadcasting!

The other book I have finished has just gone to Frere. It is called: 'Frauds or Not Frauds? Familiar Studies in Men and Crooks' and has the motto 'The English dearly love a Fraud'. I think myself it is really a stronger denunciation of the bad England than the two former ones, and I wonder if Frere will have the pluck to issue it. A very clever London cockney-Jew friend of mine who saw some of it wrote: 'Have you ever thought of asking for police protection?' You see, they can't say I'm not more native English than they are. Through parish registers I can trace unbroken descent of English yeoman farmers to a Richard Aldington, who held land of the Abbot of Evesham in 1500. What is more the name occurs in that district in Doomsday book (circa 1070) and when a relative of the Asquiths recently tried to high-hat me I told him: 'When your ancestors arrived at Hastings without landing permits, mine met the boat, and died round the last native English King of England.' He didn't like it. I don't know that I did have ancestors there, but I presume the Saxon porkers rallied round the Saxon King!

It is very pleasant to know that the Duttons are sending you the Sydney Bulletin, which (I remember) Lorenzo always praised. They are very nice young people, perhaps a little too monied and successful for us who were thankful to get a roast rabbit as a treat, but I like them very much, and they have been so kind to Catha. We spent Xmas 1954 in Firenze with them. Poveri noi! I think I shall never go to Italy again, it is too painful to see it bullied into an imitation America. Italy has no real freedom—it is simply 'a play-ground' for los Yanquis.

What has happened to Lorenzo's pictures? I am told some of them are to be exhibited at 'The Eastwood Centre', and I always thought they were released by the police on condition they were taken out of England and never returned? They should be kept together and hung in a little gallery of their own.

To-day is my day to give my fortnight 'discussion' on the

radio here with my friend F.-J. Temple, who is at last working again on his book about Lorenzo—after your Mr Pollinger insulted him and stopped him for well over a year. We talk—in French—about modern English and US writers. Recently Catha (who of course speaks French perfectly) called to me: 'Oh, do come, daddy, there's an Englishman trying to talk French on the Paris radio, and he has a <u>much</u> worse English accent than you have'. I listened to him, and indeed hope she is right.

Yes, that Edward Nehls was a burden—I did all I could for him, but his book, like that other man's—Moore is his name?—is nothing really to do with L.—it is simply a means to get the writer or compiler an academic job in USA. The Americans care nothing for art and literature, and have no literary integrity, no disinterested devotion.

I did a bit on the radio here to try to help Ezra, but they won't let him free. They hate art too much, though to be sure he isn't any great shakes at that.

Catha joins me in love to Angie and yourself—she still remembers the piggie at the ranch and Angie on horseback,

Richard

[Aldington eventually became a good friend of Moore's and also wrote a friendly preface to one of the three volumes of Nehls's *Composite Biography* of Lawrence.

The present editors deplore Frieda's occasional outbursts of anti-Semitism in these letters, which were uncharacteristic of her conversation.—eds]

Epilogue

From Frieda and from Angelo Ravagli to Mrs Hazel
Guggenheim McKinley:

Port Isabel
Texas
21 January 1951

Dear Hazel,
   You see we are here—I have a little house here on the Gulf
of Mexico—It's warm and peaceful, but not exciting.
Brownsville is our nearest town, Mexico across the border. It
might amuse you for a little while—. There are some places in
Port Isabel where you could stay.
   I am supposed to write another book but don't work hard
enough—I hope you are well and cheerful, in spite of an
uncheerful world.
   We are 5 miles out of Port Isabel, <u>Laguna Vista</u>. It's a sign on
the way to Port Isabel.
   If you feel like driving down, it would be fun to see you—

Sincerely as ever
Frieda

Dear Hazel,
   Will be nice to see you again after so long. We are in the
telephone book, that is 6001. F2-2- Port Isabel—If you phone
when you are closer I will tell you the right directions to get
here—

Angie—

[This letter is to Hazel Guggenheim McKinley, a painter whose husband,
also a painter, was an Air Force pilot, Lt Charles McKinley, killed in a plane

138

crash. In a letter of 1941, printed in E. W. Tedlock Jr's *Frieda Lawrence: the Memoirs and Correspondence*, Frieda wrote of 'a young McKinley' who had painted a picture of her in Hollywood, California. A reproduction of this portrait appears as the frontispiece to the present volume.]

Index

Abbot of Evesham, 136
Ad Astra, Vence, 1, 3
'Adventure in Spain', 128
Aga Khan, 4, 48
Aldington, Catherine, xi, 76, 81, 83, 84, 85, 91, 104, 106, 108, 109, 110, 111, 113, 122, 124, 128, 136, 137
Aldington, Netta, xi, 75, 76, 77, 79, 84, 86, 98, 101, 102
Aldington, Richard, vi, xi, xii, xiii, 37, 48, 73, 96, 107, 126, 131, 136
Allenby's army, 118
Alpes-Maritimes, ix
Angell, Mr, 105
Apocalypse, 7, 21, 23, 24, 25, 26, 31, 47
Arlen, Michael, xii, 1, 2, 3, 28, 89
Asquith, Lady Cynthia, 115, 136
Asquith, the Hon. Herbert, 136
Auden, Wystan Hugh, 131, 132
Augustin, Saint, 88

Baedeker, 113
Bank of England, 121
Barney, Elvira, 60, 61
Barrow, Gen. Sir George de S., G.C.M.G., K.C.M.G., 118
'Bavarian Gentians', viii
Beardsley, Aubrey, 104
Beers, Sir Hugo de, 52
Benkovitz, Miriam J., xi
Bennett, Arnold, 122
Berck-Plage, France, 5
Berkeley Hotel, xi
Berkman, Alexander, 60
Bevin, Ernest (Labour minister), 75
Black Sparrow Press, ix
Black Sun Press, viii, ix
Bonhver, Gaston, 98
Boni, Albert, 28

Boni, Charles, 28
Boni & Seltzer, 33, 34
Boni Liveright Ltd, 1, 3, 4
Brentford, Lord, *see* Joynson-Hicks, Sir William
Brett, Dorothy, xiii, 50, 80, 89, 96, 98, 101, 130
Brewster, Achsah, 90
Brigit, *see* Patmore, Brigit
BBC, 104, 115, 126, 130, 131, 136
British War Office, 131
Brown, Everitt, 34
Brynig, Myron, 80
Bulletin (Australia), 133
'Bundles for Britain', 105
Burke, 69
Burrows, Louie (Louisa), 64
Bynner, Witter, xii, 4, 95, 100

Caesar, Julius, 111
Café Royal, 88, 122, 129
Cagnes Casa dei Logni Place du Château, 3–4
Calabrian monks, 125
Cambridge University Press, viii
Campbell, Roy, 111, 126–7, 129, 130, 131, 132
Carletto, 87
Carswell, Cath (Catherine), 57
CBE, 111
CBS, 124
Chambers, Jessie, xiii, 90, 99
Chaplin, Charlie, 123
Chatto & Windus Ltd, 75
Chesterfield, Philip Dormer Stanhope, Earl of, 127
Churchill, Randolph, 127
Churchill, Stella, 63
Churchill, Winston, 99, 105, 108, 113, 114, 116, 127, 128

140

Churchillism, 130
Cicero, 111
Clarke, Ada Lawrence, vi, ix, x, 20, 26, 43, 44–70 *passim*
Clarke, Herbert, vi
Clarke, Jack, 46, 47, 48, 51, 52, 53, 54, 56, 57, 58, 64, 67, 89
Clift, Montgomery, 101, 102
Coca-Cola, 104, 124, 128, 133
Collected Letters of D. H. Lawrence, The, viii
Collins, Alan, 88, 116
Collins, Algernon L., 12, 16
Composite Biography (1957–9), vii, 137n
Comstock Lode, 89
'Corriere della Sera', 133
Cripps, Sir Stafford, 93
Croix de guerre, 122
Crosby, Caresse, ix, 4, 38, 39, 40, 41
Crosby, Harry, ix, 38, 39, 40, 41
Crotch, Eddie, 68
Crotch, Martha Gordon, ix, x, 35, 42–70 *passim*
'Culture', 113
Cunard, Nancy, 107, 109, 110
Curtis Brown Ltd, xiii, 1, 3, 6, 11, 12, 23, 34, 88

Daily Mail (London), 100, 117, 130
Daily Sketch (London), 117, 130
Daily Telegraph, 117, 118
D'Annunzio, 128
'Darkness at Noon', 128
Davidson, Jo, 9, 28
Death of a Hero, xi, 79
Delarue, Detective-Inspecteur, 117
der Mondt, 128
Dieterle, William, 96, 97
Doolittle, Hilda, xi, 75, 98, 100, 102
Douglas, Norman, x, xi, xii, 31, 37, 74, 81, 87, 90, 95, 103, 104, 105, 106, 107, 109, 110, 112, 126, 129, 130, 134, 135
Douglas, Robin, 82
Doyle, Charles, xii
Duell, Charles, 95
Duell, Sloan and Pearce, 96
Dunlop, Sir Thomas Dacre, 69

Durrell, Lawrence, xii
Dutton, Geoffrey, 125, 127, 128, 136

Eastwood, 126, 129, 132,
Eastwood Centre, The, 136
Eder, Dr David, 89
Editions des Deux Rives, 88
Eliot, T. S., 90, 92
'Empress of Taos', *see* Luhan, Mabel Dodge
Escaped Cock, The, viii, ix, 4, 28, 38, 40, 41, 69
Everyman, 46

Field Roscoe & Co., 54, 58
Fontana Vecchia, 99
Forte di Marmi, 19
'Fox, The', 102
Foyle, Christina, 116
Francis of Assisi, 88
'Frauds or Not Frauds? Familiar Studies in Men and Crooks', 136
Frere, A. S., xii, 27, 28, 29, 50, 61, 75, 90, 91, 101, 103, 104, 106, 107, 109, 110, 111, 112–13, 114, 116, 132, 136
Frere, Pat, xiii, 116
Frieda Lawrence: the Memoirs and Correspondence, 139n

Galsworthy, John, 92
Garnett, Edward, vii, 71, 72
Garsington, xiii
'Gastione', 24, 25
Gates, Norman T., xi
German Fleet, 130
Giglioli, Dr, 103
Giraud, 49
Goldman, Emma, 57, 60
Goodwin, Walter, 96, 97
Gordon, Peter, 43, 63
Grand Fleets, 130
Gregorovius, 103
Grey, Cecil, 93
Grove Press, 108
Gwenn, Edmund, 102

Hardy, Thomas, 27, 28, 29

Harmsworth, 48
Harper, Raymond, 41
Harris, Mrs Frank 60
Hart, B. H. Liddell, 118
Heard, Gerald, 80
Heinemann, William, 93
Heldentod, 85, 121
H. D., *see* Doolittle Hilda
Hilton, Enid, 35, 36
Hitler, Adolf, 92
Hohenlohe, Ursula von, 120
Hollywood, 32, 78, 120, 123, 139n
Holy Family, 64
Hotel Imperial, Vienna, 22
Houghton Mifflin Co., 108
Hubble, Edwin, 115
Hubble, Grace, 115
Huxley, Aldous, viii, 5, 6, 7, 9, 11,
    13, 17, 19, 20, 25, 37, 61, 63, 72,
    73, 78, 82, 87, 91, 96, 98, 100, 115,
    119, 120, 130, 132
Huxley, Julian, 88
Huxley, Maria, 61, 80, 91, 115,
    118–19, 132
Huxley, Matthew, 132

Ida (German nurse), 119, 124, 129,
    132
Illustrated News (London), 117, 130
'Inselschiff', 93
Isartal, 32

Jaffe-Richthofen, Dr Else, 113, 120
Johnson, Dr, 108
Johnson, Samuel, 127
Joyce, James, 100
Joynson-Hicks, Sir William, Lord
    Brentford, 117
Julia (peasant girl), 134

Kangaroo, 89
Keats, John, viii
Kennan's House, London, 14
Kershaw, Alister, xiii, 92, 102, 117,
    127, 132
King, Willy, 107
Kingsley Hotel, London, 28, 36
Kiowa Ranch, Taos, New Mexico,
    30, 33, 50, 70, 85, 86

Kitchener, Horatio Herbert, Lord
    Kitchener of Khartoum, 128
Koch, David, vi
Köstler, Arthur, 128
Koteliansky, S. S. ('Kot'), xiii, 57, 68,
    89
Krenkow, Fritz, 57
Krishnamurti, 80
Krug, Emil, 97

Lacy, Gerald, viii
Lady Chatterley's Lover, viii, x, 1, 4, 6,
    7, 8, 9, 10, 11, 12, 13, 18, 22, 24,
    25, 28, 31, 32, 33, 35, 37, 54, 75,
    96, 97, 98, 101, 104, 108, 117, 119,
    122, 123
Lahr, Charles, 34, 36
La Patrie, 122
*Large Collection of Unpublished Holo-
    graph Letters of Norman Douglas, A*,
    106
Last Poems (Lawrence), 107
Lawrence, D. H., vii, viii, ix, xii, xiii,
    5, 6, 8, 13, 14, 20, 22, 23, 24, 27,
    30, 35, 36, 38, 39, 40, 41, 42, 50,
    62, 66, 71–2, 80, 82, 88, 89, 91, 93,
    94, 95, 97, 98, 100, 101, 102, 103,
    104, 105, 106, 107, 109, 110, 119,
    121, 122, 125, 126, 128, 130, 132,
    134; D. H. Lawrence Centre, 112;
    Lawrence's Estate, vi, x, 14–15,
    52, 53–4; Lawrence's letters, 30,
    35, 129; Lawrence's mss, 10, 28,
    32, 96; Lawrence's pictures, 136;
    Lawrence's poems, 49, 77, 79
Lawrence, Frieda, vi, ix, xii, 15,
    42–70 *passim*, 138
Lawrence, George, x, 18, 21, 23, 24,
    31, 34, 44, 51, 52, 54, 56, 59, 60,
    62, 63, 68, 73
Lawrence, T. E. ('of Arabia'), 113,
    118, 120, 125, 127, 131, 135
*Lawrence of Arabia: A Biographical
    Inquiry*, xi, 105, 108, 110, 111, 133
Le Donne devono lavorare, 85
Les Aspras, Vence, 22, 29
Letters of D. H. Lawrence, The, viii
Light on a Dark Horse, 131
Lisk's book, 113

List Verlag, 121
Literary Guild, 87
'Lorenzo in Taos', 56
'Love of Comrades, The', 94
Lowell, Amy, xi
Lucas, Robert, viii
Luce, Elaine, 134
Luhan, Mabel Dodge, xiii, 50, 56, 80, 89, 130, 132
Lyle, Rob, 126

MacCarthy, Sir Desmond, 131
McCarthy Joseph, 111
Mackenzie, Sir ('Monty') Compton, xii, 92, 107, 108
McKinley, Charles, vi, 138–9n
McKinley, Hazel Guggenheim, vi, 138–9
MacNiven, Ian S., xi
Maestracci, Dr, 49, 62
Magnus, Maurice, 93
Mansfield, Katherine, xii, 88, 90
Man who Died, The, viii, 93
Mariani, Grado, 126, 129
Marquier, Anna, 89
Marsh, Eddie, 74, 128
Maugham, William Somerset ('Willy'), 74, 113
Meade, Mr, 11
Mecklenburgh Square, 134
Medley, Mr, 54, 61, 62, 90
Memoirs and Correspondence, viii
Memoirs of a Bookseller, 90
Merivale, Lord, 62
Minkoff, George Robert, vi
Le Miroir de l'Histoire, 117
Mistral, 121, 135
Morland, Dr, 1
Mondadori, Alberto, 85, 87, 95, 97, 110, 121, 123–4, 128, 129
Montaigne, 93, 94, 102
Monty, *see* Weekley, Montague
Moore, Harry T., vii, viii, xi, 56, 57, 58, 64, 90, 98, 101, 137
Morrell, Lady Ottoline, xiii, 61, 115, 118
'Moving Along', 107
Murry, John Middleton, xii, 8, 46, 57, 62, 64, 68, 94, 101

Murti, Krishna (Krishnamurti), 80
Musical Chairs, 94
Mussolini, Benito, 133

Napoleon, 99, 110, 118
NBC, 99
Needham, Emily (Lawrence), x, 54, 59, 60, 63
Nehls, Edward, vii, 134, 137
New York Times, xi, 98
Nichols, Robert, 89
Nogales, General, 127, 131
Noir et Blanc, 117
North Sea, 130
Not I, But the Wind . . . , viii, 89
Nottingham Guardian, 101
Nottingham University, vii

Old Bailey dock, 116
Orioli, Douglas, xi
Orioli, G. A., viii, xi, 4, 7, 8–10, 13, 16, 17, 19, 20, 21, 24, 25, 26, 27, 28, 31, 37, 38, 47, 48, 51, 53, 63, 73, 74, 82, 87, 89, 90, 103, 104, 105, 107, 109, 110, 123, 124, 126, 128, 130, 131

Padre Island, 114, 119, 132
Patmore, Brigit, 57, 75, 126, 129
Payne, Tessie, 45
Peacock Press, The 136
Peasant Pottery Shop, Vence, ix
Penguin Books Ltd, 90, 96, 97, 102
Perry, Mrs, 69
Pétain, Henri Philippe, 124
Peterson, Kenneth, vi
'Phantasia' ('Fantasia'), 92
Philips, Mr, 44, 45, 50
Pierce, Kate, 133
Pierce, General, 133
Pinorman, xi, 103, 104, 107, 108, 110, 111, 113, 126, 130
Plutarch, 98
Pollinger, Gerald, vi, xiii
Pollinger, Laurence, xiii, 1, 2, 3, 9, 10, 18, 20, 50, 51, 52, 59, 89, 93, 97, 98, 99, 113, 137
Pompey, 111
Portable D. H. L., 100–1

Port Isabel, 138
Portrait of a Genius, But . . ., 98, 127
Poujade, 133, 135
Pound, Ezra, xii, 134, 137
Prentice, Charles, 75, 82
Priestley, J. B (Jack), 82
Priest of Love: A Life of D. H. Lawrence, The, vii

Radio France, 117
Rainbow, The, viii, 64, 90
Rananim, 122
Ravagli, Angelo, x, xii, 50, 70, 71–2, 77, 79, 80, 81, 91, 105, 106, 108, 110, 111, 114, 115, 119, 120, 125, 128, 129, 135, 137, 138
Ravagli, Signora, 50
Reeves, A. S. Frere, *see* Frere, A. S.
Rejected Guest, 85
Richthofen, Baron von, vii
Richthofen, Elsa (Mrs Seaman), 18, 62, 69
Richthofen, Joanna von, xiii, 88, 91, 94, 96
Roberts, Warren, vi, 112
Robinson, Percy, 11, 12, 14, 15, 54
Rogers, Millicent, 98, 101
Rosenbach, Edward, 6, 7, 9, 11
Roth, Samuel, 33, 34, 36, 37
Rothschild, Philippe de, 98, 99, 101
Rubinstein, Helena, viii, 2, 21, 31
Russell, Bertrand, 47, 53, 55, 58, 90, 104–5, 115

Schorer, Mark, 108
Seaman, Mrs Elsa, *see* Richthofen, Elsa
Secker, Martin, 23, 51, 54, 64
Sedgwick, 50
Seldes, George, 18
Seltzer, Thomas, 1, 3, 4
Seven against Reeves, 85
Shakespeare, William, 134
Shaw, George Bernard, 63
'Ship of Death, The', viii, 83
Sims, 136
'Snake', viii
Snow, C. P. (Lord), 85
Sons and Lovers, viii, xiii, 90, 96, 99,

100, 101, 113, 120, 123
Son of Woman, 46
Southern Illinois University Press, 135
Spender, Stephen, 100, 131, 132
'Spirit of Place', 111
S. S. *Conte Grande*, 44
Sun, 40
Sydney *Bulletin*, 89, 136

'Talking Bronco', 131
Taos, New Mexico, 94
Tedlock, E. W., viii, 139n
Temple, F.-J., xiii, 110, 111, 137
This Quarter, ix, 27
Thomas, Lowell, 120, 124, 135
Thysson, 49
Time and Tide, 106, 109
The Times (London), 63, 100, 134
The Times Literary Supplement (London), 52, 107
Titus, Edward, vi, viii, ix, xiii, 1, 21
Titus, Mrs, *see* Rubinstein, Helena
Trevor-Roper, Hugh, xi
Turner, Reginald, 82, 104, 107, 126, 129

Vence, France, vii
Victoria, Queen, 87
Viking Press, 77, 79, 85, 87, 90, 93
Villa Beau Soleil, 38
Villa Robermond, 4, 39
Virgin and the Gipsy, The, 16
Vol d'Essai, 122
VUE, 122

Wadsworth, Beaumont, 101
Wallace, Edgar, xiii
Wallace, Pat (Mrs Frere), 116
Warren Gallery, London, ix
Watson, Leau, 11, 12
Weekley, Barbara, 2, 3, 4, 5, 8, 18, 20, 39, 47, 49, 50, 61, 62, 69, 70, 71
Weekley, Ernest, 61
Weekley, Montague (Monty), 62, 69
Weekley-Richthofen, Frieda, *see* Lawrence, Frieda
White, William, 93

Wilkinson, Gair, 49

William Heinemann Ltd, xii, 51, 52, 82

Williams, Tennessee, 96, 102

Williamson, Henry, 134

Windsor, Duke of, 102

Women in Love, viii, xiii, 88, 90

Yorke, Dorothy, xiii, 19, 20, 135

Young Lorenzo, 51, 53, 56

You Touched Me, 94, 102

Zeitlin, Jacob, xiii, 113